"If Peter Drucker and Mr. Rogers had a baby, his name would be Richard Sheridan. *Chief Joy Officer* is the perfect blend of irrefutable management theory and irresistible human decency. Sheridan confronts you with the elevated purpose of leadership your MBA professors didn't have the guts or clarity to teach you." —**Joseph Grenny, coauthor of** *Crucial Conversation:* ***Tools for Talking When Stakes are High*** **and** *Influencer:* ***The New Science of Leading Change***

"Through captivating stories and remarkable authenticity, Rich takes us on a journey of how to build high-performance organizations on a cultural foundation of hope, love, and joy." —**Scott DeRue, dean at the Ross School of Business, University of Michigan**

"What others call inspirational or even aspirational leadership concepts, Richard Sheridan calls the Joy of Leadership. It's encoded in Menlo's very DNA." —**Sam MacPherson, founder of The Lean Leadership Academy and Green Beret Way Leadership Experience**

"*Chief Joy Officer* is a tour de force in how you can become a positive leader. You will understand why positive leadership produces more payoffs than any other approach." —**Robert E. Quinn, Ross School of Business, Center for Positive Leadership**

"Richard Sheridan shows leaders how they can leave fear behind and lead from a place of service and joy." —**Raj Sisodia, cofounder and chairman emeritus, Conscious Capitalism International**

"For many, work is suffering. It doesn't have to be that way. Rich Sheridan tells us how to be the person who makes that happen—no matter where we are in our organizations." —**Wayne Baker, professor of Management and Organizations, University of Michigan Ross School of Business and Center for Positive Organizations**

"Read this book and you will want to be a Chief Joy Officer. Inspiring lessons from an exceptional leader of a company built on joy." —**Jeffrey Liker, author of** *The Toyota Way*

"Like a hip consumer product, the organizational design at Menlo Innovations epitomizes great design—a simple intuitive look and feel, based on universal principles, and underpinned by sophisticated approaches to management systems, personal development, and leadership." —Andy Eichfeld, former leader of the Lean Management practice at McKinsey

"Rich Sheridan is a masterful storyteller who reframes what it means to be a leader at work. For him, joy isn't about happiness. It's about purpose." —Michael Pacanowsky, Gore-Giovale Chair in Business Innovation, Westminster College

"A good leader has an obligation to create an inclusive and energizing environment, filled with authenticity, humility, transparency, and an iron resolve to drive fear and intimidation out of the organization—all shared in a way that only a master storyteller like Rich can." —Jim Morgan, senior advisor at the Lean Enterprise Institute, coauthor of *Designing the Future*, and former Ford global engineering director

"Richard Sheridan has a great attitude for succeeding in business and life! If you take care of your people, they will take care of everything else that matters. The ONE thing—the ONLY—thing is people." —Heidi Musser, executive vice president and principal consultant at Leading Agile, retired VP and CIO at USAA

"This book is a recipe for humble, effective leadership . . . follow it and you will have a positive, fear-free, trusting, fun, and, most of all, productive workplace." —Ron Sail, former leader GE global employee services and chief cultural anthropologist at The Alchemy Group

"Richard Sheridan has cracked the code: You can lead young people by fear or passion—and fear doesn't work. If you give them your all, they'll give you everything. Sheridan shows you how, and why." —John U. Bacon, *New York Times* bestselling author of *Bo's Lasting Lessons*

"*Work* and *joy* are two words most people wouldn't associate with each other, but Rich Sheridan isn't like most people. It may challenge many of your common assumptions about business, and it will certainly make your mind spin with new ideas and possibilities." —**Jim Ferrell, author and managing partner at the Arbinger Institute**

"We can all learn from the approaches and concepts in this book. We can all become more authentic, courageous leaders who bring gratitude, optimism, and belief to their work . . . every day." —**Jack Salzwedel, chair and CEO of American Family Insurance**

"Focusing on *how* people work more than the content of their work is possibly *the* main aspect of a leader's job. But Rich's story stretches further. You are what you think, and in struggling to practice this approach you the leader gets developed. Your customer, your team . . . they help *you* grow." —**Mike Rother, author of *Toyota Kata* and *The Toyota Kata Practice Guide***

"Full of insightful personal stories, *Chief Joy Officer* is a unique guide to what it takes to create joy in the workplace, from someone who has successfully done that at Menlo Innovations." —**Steve Denning, author of *The Age of Agile***

"Finally! A candid and humble leadership book packed with the degree of emotion that has forever been the key to outstanding leadership, but largely ignored." —**Karen Martin, author of *Clarity First* and *The Outstanding Organization***

"If it's true the country should be run more like a business, the next president would do well to start by selecting Rich Sheridan to be our Chief Joy Officer." —**Ari Weinzweig, cofounding partner, Zingerman's Community of Businesses and author of *Zingerman's Guide to Good Leading***

"*Chief Joy Officer* is a clear articulation of the values that leaders must embody and practice to attain what's been referred to as 'servant leadership' over the years." —**Vijay Sankaran, technology leader, Ann Arbor, Michigan**

"Many business books provide the ingredients for success; vision, purpose, servant leadership, empowerment, and great culture. Rich shows you how to mix it all together, providing the perfect recipe for joyful success for both you and your team."   **—Mike Altendorf, retired CIO of Do it Best Corp**

"Rich Sheridan lays out a standard of excellence that leaders of all types should aspire to no matter what title they may hold. In the process, he has significantly raised the bar for every leader and every company—and done us all a great service.   **—Bo Burlingham, author of *Small Giants* and *Finish Big***

CHIEF JOY OFFICER

CHIEF Joy OFFICER

How Great Leaders Elevate Human Energy and Eliminate Fear

RICHARD SHERIDAN

FOREWORD BY TOM PETERS,
AUTHOR OF *IN SEARCH OF EXCELLENCE*

PORTFOLIO/PENGUIN

Portfolio/Penguin
An imprint of Penguin Random House LLC
375 Hudson Street
New York, New York 10014

Most Portfolio books are available at a discount when purchased in quantity for sales promotions or corporate use. Special editions, which include personalized covers, excerpts, and corporate imprints, can be created when purchased in large quantities. For more information, please call (212) 572–2232 or e-mail specialmarkets@penguinrandomhouse.com. Your local bookstore can also assist with discounted bulk purchases using the Penguin Random House corporate Business-to-Business program. For assistance in locating a participating retailer, e-mail B2B@penguinrandomhouse.com.

ISBN: 9780735218222 (hardcover)
ISBN: 9780735218239 (ebook)

Printed in the United States of America
10 9 8 7 6 5 4 3 2 1

Book design by Daniel Lagin

With love to Carol,

Despite your dislike of roller coasters,
you've gladly joined me for the ride of a lifetime.

To my best friend, James,

This story would never have come true without your partnership.

CONTENTS

PART II
Building a Culture of Joyful Leadership

FOREWORD

I URGE YOU TO DISTRUST WHAT I'M WRITING. THAT IS ONE ODD-ball way to start a foreword, right? Well, my point is that I got a stiff neck reading Rich Sheridan's book. The stiff neck came from nodding—nodding vigorously—at damn near every line. What can I say, I agree with virtually every word—and, more important, every sentiment—expressed in *Chief Joy Officer*. I am, in short, not an unbiased observer able to give a balanced preview of what lies between this book's front and back covers.

I am writing as a fan and a believer. And a believer in the personal and strategic importance of this book.

I am, like most who do what I do, appalled by the statistics that consistently show that only about one-third of workers are satisfied with their job. That is a great human tragedy. Unless you are born with a sterling silver spoon, you will spend the majority of your waking hours as an adult at work. To be in constant despair about your work situation is, literally, to throw your life away.

Think about it.

Please.

Rich Sheridan is even more appalled than I am. I don't think it needs to be that way, and he doesn't think it needs to be that way. In *Chief Joy Officer* he gives us a viable—and proven—path out of the mess that typically constitutes a day (life!) at the office.

This is above the bottom line. This is above the top line—a new top of the top line perhaps. Rich's founding partner, James Goebel, did an assessment of what made for great employees at Menlo Innovations. From that assessment came three guiding principles:

"Create meaningful, positive human impact."

"Always demonstrate integrity and authenticity."

"Act in a way that expresses care, hope, love, and joy."

What a menu! And Menlo's record of success in the toughest industry around says to you and me that it is not pie in the sky. It can be done, done very effectively—and sustained.

This is a relatively short book. But it will, I hope, take you a long time to read. To "get it" requires continued reflection and a deep, frank personal assessment of where you've been, where you are, where you want to go, and who you want to be. It will benefit from conversations with your spouse, your colleagues, your dear uncle Arthur, your teenage kids. This is a book about how you live your life and interact with your teammates. Just like they say about old age (trust me on this), it ain't for sissies. To read *Chief Joy Officer* without reflection is to miss 95 percent of the point.

I've given about twenty-five hundred presentations—and virtually every one features PowerPoint slides. About eighteen months ago, to celebrate the fiftieth anniversary of my first management job (junior U.S. Navy officer—a Seabee—in Vietnam), I decided to pull the best of my slides together into what we called, internally, MOAP/the Mother of All Presentations. It ended up running to 4,096 slides with 100,000-plus words of annotation. Well, only one slide could be the first slide, right? So I needed one single solo slide to summarize fifty years' worth of gut-busting work. The prize went to the crazy entrepreneur Richard Branson:

"Business has to give people enriching, rewarding lives, or it's not worth doing."

That was it, No. 1 of 4,096. And I think that simple quote captures my view of the world almost perfectly—and captures Rich Sheridan's view as well. Though Rich is a youngster by my standard, I sometimes think when I read his work that we were twins separated at birth.

For what it's worth—and I think it's worth a lot—the runner-up to Branson for the number one slot came from the late Robert Altman, the film director. Upon winning a lifetime achievement Oscar, he said, among other things, "The role of the director is to create a space where the actors and actresses can become more than they've ever been before, more than they've dreamed of being." Bingo! And once again the de facto subtext of *Chief Joy Officer.*

All of this, it is imperative to add, takes on special urgency in the face of the change we will confront in the near future. One Oxford study suggests that fully 50 percent of American white-collar jobs are at risk to artificial intelligence in the next twenty years. And that includes the *high end* of the labor force. As Nicholas Carr said in *The Glass Cage: Automation and Us,* "The intellectual talents of highly trained professionals are no more protected from automation than is the driver's left turn."

While there is dramatic disagreement among very smart people about the timing of "all this," to my mind change of this nature introduces a new, moral imperative into enterprise management— right now. Here is the way I stated the challenge in my latest book, *The Excellence Dividend*:

"Your principal moral obligation as a leader is to develop the skill set, 'soft' and 'hard,' of every one of the people in your charge to the maximum extent of your abilities."

That is, "extreme people development" moves up from a "smart thing to do" to a first-order moral imperative that cannot or must not be evaded or avoided—starting this afternoon, not tomorrow morning or next week. (Incidentally, in the book I anoint "training and development" as "Capital Investment #1.")

The substance and spirit of *Chief Joy Officer*, then, is timeless— *and* timely. Clearly, the attributes that will allow us to survive— and, one hopes, thrive—in the decade(s) ahead are the attributes that animate and are so wonderfully addressed in this book.

Remember from above:

"Act in a way that expresses care, hope, love, and joy."

Business is about people.

Damn it!

Business is about caring about people, respecting people, helping people grow—helping people grow beyond their wildest dreams and grow as good people.

Back to those dratted slides of mine. One features a tombstone. And it reads:

James T. Jones

23 June 1940–17 September 2017

Net worth: $17,832,776.14

The next slide says: "NO!" in hyper-big type. That is, I suggest, speaking particularly passionately as a seventy-five-year-old, that no one's tombstone features one's net worth. What one remembers in old age and, more important, what one is remembered for is not the dollars accumulated but instead the people she or he helped develop professionally and personally along the way.

Helping people grow and develop and lead more rewarding lives is the topic of this wonderful—and, to my mind, unique—book. And, by the by, it is a terrific and doable way to run a growing and profitable business of 2—or 1,002—people.

Bravo and thank you, Rich.

And bravo and thank you, Menlonians, for leading the way and showing all of us what's possible.

Tom Peters

1 March 2018

Golden Bay, New Zealand

Author of many bestselling business books on the topic of business excellence, including *In Search of Excellence* (1982) and most recently *The Excellence Dividend* (2018).

Joy Is Personal

A man is what he thinks about all day long.

—Ralph Waldo Emerson

FROM MY MIDTWENTIES TO MY EARLY FORTIES, I WORKED AT THE same place: a company called Interface Systems, on the west side of Ann Arbor, Michigan. The office was near Jackson and Zeeb roads, a twenty-minute commute from our home via I-94.

I started out as a programmer, and before long, I was asked to lead the technical efforts of programming teams. By my thirties I was no longer typing in the code alongside the people I was leading, but rather managing their efforts to create those same products. I was promoted again, then again, granted more authority and more people to manage; rewarded with raises, stock options, and a nice office; and given decision-making power. I had every-thing the world measures as success.

This time of recognition, promotions, and increasing responsibil-ity should have been the highlight of my career at the time. And yet . . .

As time passed, I also found myself sneaking out of the office earlier and earlier, as close to 5 p.m. as I could without being no-ticed. During the day, I would turn my monitor away from the door and play FreeCell, forcing mindless lulls in what should have been busy, productive days. The prospect of going to work filled me with a sense of unsettledness and dread. I started abandoning my most efficient drive down I-94 to the office, instead opting for back roads, driving past Interface farther and farther out into the Michigan country landscape before finally doubling back and driving to work.

I was burning out, and it had everything to do with my defini-tion of leadership.

The culture at Interface favored getting products out to market before they were ready and dealing with the inevitable quality problems that resulted, a process we sarcastically referred to as "just smushing it."* Everyone (executives, customers, and users) then blamed us for producing inferior products. Through my per-sistent advocating, I was eventually permitted to allocate 30 per-cent of my team's time to simply fixing problems that were coming at us every single day. And 30 percent wasn't enough. This had a demoralizing effect on everyone in the organization.

I became convinced that we just didn't have the right people to

---

* One of my most talented developers had a sign in his cube that read Just Smush-it. He would wryly smile and joke that the dash was in the wrong place.

do the job. Meetings to sort out quality problem "priorities" lasted for hours. We would decide which 10 percent of the problems we had time to address, which would be described in "release notes" (that no customer would EVER read), and which could be recast as "features" in cleverly worded but utterly incomprehensible end-user documentation. Even worse, hiding behind all the bugs was a product that couldn't actually be used by regular human beings (we enjoyed calling those people *stupid users*), and it didn't actually solve real problems for them.

I was frustrated by how little *teamwork* was at play within my various teams and the utter lack of an effective relationship between the technical team and the marketing and sales side of the house. Everything felt disorganized and chaotic. We tried so many different versions of meetings, forms, and status reporting, but nothing seemed to address the root cause of our poor communication and the disappointing results that followed. Most of my team members were heroically in charge of one piece of a complex technical product line and no one else knew what they knew, so when crunch time came, there was incessant overtime and a fear of vacations being taken by these same heroes at critical moments. Most of my team carried their maximum allowable vacation balances because they couldn't actually use it. When people did take an inevitable vacation, they were armed with laptops, cell phones, and pagers so they would be available to apply emergency fixes to their code. There was rarely an uninterrupted vacation for our technology heroes. And the pieces that each one of them was working on never easily integrated with the work of their peers. They simply could not agree on an integrated strategy, which led to inevitable fights. My introverted technical leaders seldom fought with words but rather with code. In one dramatic version of this, one of my programmers created some code that the other didn't agree with. The other programmer displayed his disagreement by changing the code to the way he thought was right. These rounds of competing edits went on for a couple of months before my boss, the CEO, called me and them into his office and declared: "Guys, you are killing the company . . . agree or else." The "or else" now seems humorous to me, as there was no "or else." If we had fired one or the other or both, we were equally screwed.

I began fantasizing about an escape, leaving Ann Arbor and corporate life to start a canoe camp in the Boundary Waters of Minnesota. My wife and my three daughters still chuckle when they hear that idea. They have no idea how serious I was.

One afternoon in October 1997, Bob Nero, the new CEO of Interface Systems, invited me into his office and told me I was being promoted to VP of R&D, a job he had been grooming me for since he arrived on the scene early in 1996. I listened patiently to this amazing offer. It took me about a minute to tell him no. I told him I didn't want to sign up for the uncapped personal commitment required of a VP of a troubled public company. My daughters were still young (thirteen, eleven, and eight) and I was afraid I'd wake up ten years later and realize I missed the best part of being a dad. The Eagle Scout in me wanted to help Bob. The provider in me wanted the financial rewards that would pay for college and eventual weddings for three beautiful and intelligent young women. Yet, I was confounded by the demons that I knew would further kill my spirit as my career stepped up a gear and a speed.

Bob was upset with me. His plans to turn the company around depended on me taking this pivotal role. He didn't have a plan B.

I went home that night and quietly thought it all through. Despite my negative thoughts, my inner optimist had not been subdued. I thought this could be my chance. From this perch, I could lead in a new way, a way that had never been done before. I was stuck in a room full of manure, and I was suddenly thrilled with the idea that there had to be a *pony* in here somewhere. It was an irrational thought, but my energy suddenly turned 180 degrees.

The next morning I told Bob I would take the job . . . on one condition: that he would support me in building the best damn software team that Ann Arbor had ever seen. Neither one of us ever looked back after that day.

At the earliest stage of this newfound mind-set, I knew there had to be a different approach to leadership. It couldn't be based on heroes. Perhaps the programmer in me believed that there was just as big of an opportunity for elegance in leadership as there was for elegance in code. Every good programmer will recall the one time they felt so proud of their technical creation, not only for what it did but also for how it was written. I began to believe the essence of true leadership involved way more *how* than *what*, and as author Simon Sinek would eventually teach us, *why*.

An age-old human argument is centered on the morality of "Does the end justify the means?" Humanity has learned and relearned that the "means" matters so much. We have seen countless examples in human history where unethical or unsupportable *means* always catch up with you, no matter how good or noble the original intended outcome. My life journey suddenly became centered on a bright, new, energizing hypothesis:

There is a *means* of leadership—as yet undiscovered or at least so uncommon as to seem quixotic—that can systematically produce *ends* that match our hope and dreams for pride, success, and delight. In short, I began to believe that a pursuit of joy was not only possible but sustainable. Later I would come to learn that joy was the only thing that truly mattered.

My Dream for Joy

If I wanted to create an environment where others and I could work with pride, I needed to find a new operating model. The one we had—and the one I saw in so many companies around Ann Arbor and around the country—wasn't working. We needed to replace the traditional model, which was marked by fear and bureaucracy, with one that allowed teams to bring their whole selves to work every day. This better model would support a collegial and productive environment, where innovation and imagination helped foster practical inventions that would serve and inspire customers. That creativity and innovation, in not just product but process, would also power the team's energy, creating a kind of human perpetual-motion machine. All of this, by the way, would pay off in real terms too, leading to higher revenues, bigger profits, and other markers of business success.

What I was seeking, which would become crystal clear later in my career, was *joy at work*. No word other than *joy* fit my engineering ideal—of designing and building something, perhaps many things, that would see the light of day and be enjoyably used and widely adopted by the people for whom it was intended. Yes, that's what I wanted above all else—joyful outcomes produced by joyful people working in a joyful place.

This is not the same as happiness, mind you. Where happiness is a momentary state of being, joy is deeper and more meaningful—and not as fleeting. You can be joyful without being happy every minute; you can be joyful when the work is difficult and challenging, even when you feel angry at the world, your team, your customers, and yourself.

Building a joyful company was my big dream. And to up the ante even more, I wanted to implement this joyful dream in an industry not exactly known for delighting customers or employees—software design. My industry coined the phrase "death march" in a business context. We were well known for all-night coding sessions and poorly managed and buggy products. What was I thinking, trying to make such radical change in a field like that? Perhaps the canoe camp *was* a good idea after all.

My journey to a better way of working started out of disillusionment and ended where I am now—as the leader of a very joyful, award-winning software company called Menlo Innovations (still based in Ann Arbor). My partners, colleagues, and I got to this place with a deliberate focus on two intertwined keys: culture and leadership. In other words, we entirely rethought how the team interacted with one another, with customers, with other stakeholders, with their work environment—this is culture. We also rethought how leaders define the company's purpose and get everyone aligned around common systems and expectations to get real work done, constantly iterating and always improving themselves, their peers and employees, and the whole team. I'd go a step further and add that we also redefined who leaders are—beyond the name on some plaque outside a corner office but rather those people who can truly inspire, motivate, and develop others, regardless of their title or position.

End Permission Seeking: No More Fear-based Leadership

I went deep into Menlo's joyful culture in my first book, *Joy, Inc.* As a result of writing the book, I got to connect with many people who wanted to institute a joyful culture in their work, in all kinds of industries, in companies large and small all around the world. I found that so many of our conversations about culture came back to leadership. People wanted to know how to be the leader who could get others to follow them to a better place. They were curious about what good leadership looked like, how it was sustained over time, and what leadership looked like as an executive, as a manager, or as a really committed employee who might not even have anyone officially reporting to them. These conversations were the impetus for this book.

Joy at work seems like such a simple idea—just make everyone happy, right? No! Embracing joy at work means fighting joy's greatest enemy: fear. And unfortunately, leadership based on fear is the status quo for nearly every organization and bureaucracy. Choosing to lead with joy is a big shift.

At Interface, fear of our shareholders drove us to ship inferior product. Fear that our programmers would screw up drove us to invent arcane systems of trying to test quality into their work. Fear that we would ship two weeks after our competitors drove us to cut every possible corner just to get something out there that simply disappointed everyone. Fear that we weren't working hard enough or smart enough led to incessant demands for overtime.

And at other companies, what is the reason for . . .

Approvals needed from leadership on all decisions? Fear that your people will screw up, that you don't have the right people?

Long memos with confining and condescending instructions? Fear that your people won't get it, that they don't care enough?

Even little moments in the workplace reek of fear. When a senior leader cuts off someone speaking at a meeting? That's the leader's fear—of being an imposter, of needing to prove his or her authority, of being "found out," or of being outshone and losing rank.

Every written formal memo about working hours, workplace attire,* etc. Yep, fear.

Every time we make a new process rule because of one bad outcome—fear.

I have good news and bad news. The good news is that it's possible to create an organization free from fear, where people bring their whole selves to work and the full range of their potential, energy, and talent is put to the company's benefit. (That's what you're paying for, isn't it?)

---

* In 2018, General Motors CEO Mary Barra boldly rewrote GM's dress code. She took the ten-page HR policy and reduced it to two words: Dress appropriately. (Way to go, Mary!)

The bad news is, the path there is anything but comfortable. It involves letting go of most of what you've learned or experienced. It means changing what you believe about the people who work for you and with you.

The best news, though, is it means getting back to your own dreams of what *you* always thought was possible. It means getting back to the truest form of who you really are and what you always believed you could become. It means getting back to your own very personal definition of joy. One you'd be proud to have written on your gravestone.

This book won't be a blueprint for a one-size-fits-all model of leadership, or for explaining which of the twenty-six leadership styles you exhibit. It is my goal to make a stand for *leading with joy* as something that you not only can do but something you MUST do. I will use tangible and practical examples from our experience at Menlo (and those of a few other companies) to show you that a more joyful, more human, more fulfilling path to leadership is not only attainable but imperative for survival. By questioning business as usual and envisioning the organization you truly want to work for or build, you'll also define the kind of life you want to lead—at work, outside of work, all together in its messy complex glory.

I want to make sure you're not taking the scenic road to work, driving back roads because you can't face the idea of showing up at the office and going through another day of disillusionment. Let's get you to a place where you bound inside those doors with enthusiasm and energy and share that with others as the leader. Where those on your team can become leaders in their own right because you've built a culture in which leadership can thrive. Let's make you a Chief Joy Officer, which isn't so much a job title as a state of mind and a way of being a different kind of leader.

I started on this leadership transformation many years ago at Interface Systems, when I decided to not let myself drift into disillusionment and escapism. I continued this journey when I, along with my cofounders, started Menlo Innovations in 2001. And I am still very much on this journey, as you'll see in these pages.

Part of embracing the joyful path to leadership means constantly assessing and pledging to do better, to improve one another and ourselves. I hope to enroll you in this work too, so that together we can build pockets of joy in business all around the world.

What Do You Believe?

It may seem idealistic, but a journey to joyful leadership starts with what you believe. You may have kept these personal beliefs buried for so long that they are no longer familiar. I can assure you . . . they are still there, waiting to be unlocked and unleashed.

You've probably encountered this quote from Gandhi:

Your beliefs become your thoughts,
Your thoughts become your words,
Your words become your actions,
Your actions become your habits,
Your habits become your values,
Your values become your destiny.

Whether or not we want to believe Gandhi's words, we all have to admit we've seen them play out over and over again. Sometimes they play out wonderfully; you've seen this positive alignment in teachers you revere, parents who raise good kids, and leaders who inspire everyone around them. I'm certain you have seen it play out the other way too.

Several years ago, my cofounder James Goebel conducted an exercise to understand our beliefs and values as a team. He met individually with nearly every Menlonian and asked them a simple question:

"If you left Menlo to start your own company, what three team members would you take along with you?"

He listened as Menlonians spoke about the others on the team they most valued and why they would choose those specific few to go with on the precarious journey of entrepreneurship. He wrote down the words they used on note cards. Afterward, he looked for patterns and began simplifying the notes into a single artifact organized by guiding principles and critical behaviors—and visible actions that give us evidence that the critical behaviors are at work—which together make up what we *value*.

From the team's answers, James identified three guiding principles, which clarify how we want to see ourselves and how we want the world to perceive us:

Create meaningful, sustainable, positive, human impact.
Always demonstrate integrity and authenticity.
Act in a way that expresses care, hope, love, and joy!

These guiding principles act as Menlo's decision-making guard-rails. We can improve the speed of decision making if we consider that each decision we make is consistent with these guiding principles. If we behave consistently with these guiding principles, there isn't much need for checking in with each other to see if we are doing the right thing.

James also codified critical behaviors and visible actions that exemplified those behaviors. Behaviors are the general norms of how we intend to act; visible actions are the leading examples of those behaviors. Now remember, this is what Menlonians were seeing in each other. Thus, while these behaviors and actions were aspirational, they were also real. This is the list James came up with based on these conversations:

Be Responsible by working with focus, being transparent, acting with discipline, and practicing servant leadership.

Be Effective by using systems thinking, simplifying, making decisions, finding compromise, and acting proactively.

Grow by fostering inquisitiveness, determining intrinsic motivation, reading, teaching, and mentoring compassionately.

Nurture Healthy Relationships by assuming good intent, putting others first, displaying empathy, bringing enthusiasm, and actively listening.

Be Willing to Enter the Danger* by displaying passion and

---

* "Enter the Danger" is a phrase we have come to love from Patrick Lencioni's book *Getting Naked.* It refers to the ability of each team member to sense danger in any

respect, engaging challenging topics with empathy, and
embracing mistakes.

Deliver Life-changing Experiences by thinking holistically,
understanding others' points of view, and passionately
embracing hard work.

Embrace Diversity by hiring first for talents, recruiting widely
and inclusively, and taking chances on people.

These are the very tangible things we value as a team. In total
they comprise the real values of our team and therefore our company. We believe they are worthy of our collective pursuit.

Now, I would love to say we operate all day every day with each
of these guiding principles, critical behaviors, and visible actions in
mind. But this side of heaven, we must still deal with regular human
beings who have challenges at home, don't feel well, get upset when
they feel disrespected or unheard, and misinterpret the actions of
others around them. In other words, we are a real team with real
people.

Our mission to "end human suffering in the world as it relates to technology"—by returning joy to technology teams and
the experiences those teams create for others—is an ongoing one.
We will never be able to say our mission is completed. So it follows that we will never be done pursuing the guiding principles, critical behaviors, and visible actions listed above. Although
they are not attainable by everyone, every day, they can serve as

---

conversation (often with customers) and be willing to step right in and deal with it
instead of delaying the difficult topic for another day.

our guiding light to a better team and better work. Inch by inch, day by day, conversation by conversation, we can get closer to and better at living in accordance to our principles and working toward our mission. Even as we make mistakes, suffer setbacks, take three steps forward and then back one or two, we are always moving toward a better version of the world and our place in it.

Constantly and consistently moving forward by applying these values is the hard work of leadership. And it must happen while we are doing real work to make payroll, cover expenses, find new customers, keep current customers happy, grow our technical skills, find new people, replace those who leave or don't work out, and still find time to enjoy our lives and our families.

Wouldn't it be enough to simply have the boss declare, "Pay attention to these values *or else*?" and then go about his or her day? We could simply require frontline staff to dutifully follow these principles, behaviors, and actions every day and remove ourselves from enforcing them. Sure, we could add behaviors or actions to the list, along with an accompanying explanation in the employee handbook. We could hold an annual refresher course and then post updated placards on the wall. We could structure performance reviews around values and say that your next raise would be determined by demonstrated adherence.

This is not enough. What we want—what we need—is for our leaders to intrinsically exhibit these values in their everyday work as an example to everyone around them. We need to live them out loud, in word and deed. Our values should be evident in how we treat each other, our customers, our vendors, and our community. They should be obvious when looking at any work we put out. And if we do this consistently, over time we will see these values beyond the workplace—in our homes, our neighborhoods, our communities, and our schools.

Can you imagine the joy that would accompany this kind of reality?

Joy, Values, and Stability

I have learned over the last many years that the word *joy* can be a difficult one to grasp in its fullness and richness, especially in the context of business. Many people ask me why joy is the overarching value at Menlo and if it implies that we are striving for constant happiness and fun every day.

At Menlo, we find joy in the hard work we do together. It would be impossible to be happy every minute of every day. Are we happy? At times, of course we are, maybe even most days. Do we have fun? Yup. There is laughter every day at Menlo. We never take ourselves too seriously. Yet, joy transcends the happiness, the fun, the profits, the sales, the technology, and the growth. Joy is about the profound change we are trying to make in the world. In order to get there we must employ every ounce of the best part of ourselves every minute we can. We will not be perfect at it, but we need to identify joy even in the difficult pursuit.

Seeking joy by itself won't work. You need to tie joy to values— to seed joy in guiding principles, behaviors, and actions. If you do, though, you'll set the groundwork for momentum in your work and for positive stability that will help you sustain high performance (and a high level of joy) for everyone your company interacts with.

An airplane is designed to take flight and stay stable, even in poor weather and turbulence. As a pilot, I was taught that positive stability is the foundation of modern aircraft design. If you are flying along straight and level and turbulence buffets your craft, the plane is designed to get back into straight and level flight without pilot intervention. In fact, trying to overcontrol the aircraft can be dangerous.

If the aircraft is designed correctly, the act of piloting requires less effort. Then your primary job becomes to chart the course, check the waypoints, monitor the fuel, and guard against emergencies, which, if you've done everything else you're supposed to do (annual maintenance, diligence of preflight checklists, and paying attention to key indicators like fuel levels), will be rare to nonexistent. When conditions are right, you can simply take in the beauty of the flight itself, realizing that you are enjoying one of mankind's most impressive engineering achievements.

Of course, things don't always go so well that the aircraft will simply take care of itself without skilled and practiced intervention. Weather changes suddenly, equipment malfunctions, mistakes are made. We must be prepared and vigilant. We must act when conditions warrant action.

Leaders are like pilots. They are responsible for a lot, but they can't do their jobs safely entirely by themselves. They depend on help from others and are aided by systems that keep them as safe as possible while allowing them to get where they are going.

Strong values provide this positive stability to our organizations. While we are doing all the frontline work of the business, the core culture is nurtured and maintained somewhat routinely like any ingrained habit. It's not really *that* easy, but running an organization becomes a whole lot harder when we don't know how to judge ourselves in any given situation or understand what makes our company unique and what our path is. Values and guiding principles gently push us back on course when the difficult clients or hard economic times attempt to divert us from our mission.

In the chapters that make up part 1, we will go beyond the core company values I shared above to dive into our most precious *leadership* values, those that we most aspire to in order to become the best leaders we can and to foster the growth of joyful leaders within our team. You might think, *Really? In addition to the core values, there are also* leadership *values?* Yes, much like the difference between being a member of a family versus being a parent in that family, the values of an organization and its members and the values of leaders are not one and the same. We'll explore what it means to lead an organization and take on the awesome responsibility of guiding, supporting, and protecting those around you.

Part 2 is about putting those values into practice to create a culture of joyful leadership. We'll look at the importance of distilling purpose, the difference between bosses and leaders, and how we approach systems thinking, caretaking, learning, and storytelling to build a high-functioning organization. We'll also dive into what it means to work efficiently without traditional hierarchy, and why it's a more human way to work.

I now know that a leadership journey is a learning journey that's never done. I am blessed to have so many friends around the world who have joined me on this journey to joy. They regularly point me to other leaders whose books and talks inspire them. This further enhances my own learning journey. At the end of the book, I've included a list of favorite resources and sources of personal inspiration. I encourage you to check these out—and to create your own and share your joy with others far and wide.

PART I

What Are Joyful Leaders?

CHAPTER 1

Authentic

The privilege of a lifetime is to become who you truly are.

—C. G. Jung

SO LET'S START SOMEWHERE A BIT SCARY AND DEFINITELY PER-sonal. Who do you say you are, through words and actions, to the outside world?

The very idea of being authentic can be a difficult one to grasp and hold on to. We must learn to confront the mask we so comfortably wear to work every day. Only then can we recognize how different this mask makes us from our true inner self—that person, in our quiet moments, who grapples between our deeply seated values and the messy details of work and life.

Own Your Mask

There is a wonderful nonprofit in Michigan called Ele's Place. It was named for a baby girl, Ele Stover, who died at eleven months old and left behind a grieving family, including four siblings who had great difficulty processing the painful loss of their youngest sister.

At Menlo, we often hold "Lunch and Learns," bringing different leaders from the community into our office and engaging with them over a brown bag lunch. The leadership team of Ele's Place came into Menlo for one of these Lunch and Learns to share their history and their work in ending the silent suffering of those grieving the loss of a family member.

They walked us through their program, explaining the activities they offer family members, particularly children, to connect with others who have suffered similar loss. One of the exercises they do with their group members is to create laminated place mats with drawings of their loved ones' favorite meals, so they could still share dinnertime with the lost sibling or parent. It was so touching to hear how this helped kids navigate their grief and we were all moved by what was written on each of these thoughtful creations. Reading "I miss you, Dad" tore me up inside as I thought of my own daughters.

The most poignant artifacts the Ele's Place team brought with them were hard white plastic masks, similar to those you might see at a costume party. Each mask was personalized by the young, grieving family members. On the outside of the mask, the kids—typically teens figuring out how to express their confusing swirl of feelings— would write the emotions they hoped the rest of the world would see, things like "I'm doing OK," "I'm better now," "I'm fine," "I've moved on," or even just "Happy," "Fun," or other positive emotions. On the inside of the masks, they wrote what they truly felt, those emotions they didn't feel comfortable sharing with the public. Those words were very different: "When will the pain go away?" "Why God?" "Lonely," "Scared," "Hurting," "Abandoned," "Bitter," "Lost," "Guilty," or "Angry."

As the Ele's Place team explained to us, the teens shared the inside of their masks with each other. Of course, many of the same words and phrases showed up on everyone's "inside masks." For the first time since their loss, these teens realized that others shared their feelings, which allowed them to open up in new ways and begin to authentically process their broken hearts.

I think sharing the inside of our masks is the hardest part of authenticity, especially for leaders. On the outside, the mask of a leader would likely say "Strong," "Successful," "Confident," "Competent," "Ambitious," "In charge," or other words we believe the world wants us to be. But what does a leader's mask say on the inside? "Scared?" "Worried?" "Overwhelmed?" "Stressed?" "Unprepared?" I know mine would. And I bet our masks would look a lot more similar than we've ever really acknowledged.

Bringing Our Whole Self to Work

Is this desire to present a better face to the world than the one we see in ourselves a necessary component of leadership? Do we really want to expose our most vulnerable selves to those we lead?

I believe authenticity is less about putting on display the full range of emotions we experience every day and more about sharing our masks so our teams can see who we really are. How many of us are one person at home and a completely different person at work? This may be the biggest danger of the modern workplace: that we are practically forced to live a lie most of our waking hours and then we go home to self-medicate—literally or figuratively—to avoid looking at our side of the mask. Like the grieving teens at Ele's Place, we can't begin to heal from the stress of presenting a false face at work until we realize how many of us are doing the same thing and experiencing the same feelings of fear, uncertainty, inadequacy, and so on.

The "living lie" culture of workplaces is often rooted in the idea that what is happening outside of work must be compartmentalized and denied in order to be seen as the perfect employee or boss at work. Work then becomes the place to pretend that those other realities don't exist. This starts early in our careers and often accelerates as we move up the ladder. Often, those who succeed rapidly are seen as *universally* available to work. Their personal lives aren't just in the back seat but locked in the trunk, gagged and bound.

To develop ourselves as leaders we need to bring ourselves to work. Our whole selves, trouble and all.

A few years ago, one of our team members was struggling with his health for some time. He was due to have surgery to remove a dangerous tumor. He shared this news with James and me and asked for it to remain private, which we understood and honored. But he then decided independently to share the news with the team, as he would be gone for the foreseeable future to heal and hopefully recover from his surgery. He took the floor at our daily standup meeting to share how scared he was about the upcoming surgery. One team member, Eric S., reacted to this shocking news by walking up to that brave employee and giving him a hug. It warmed my heart beyond words to see we created an environment where this kind of outpouring of compassion could be offered publicly and without hesitation.

Authenticity doesn't only need to come at moments of crisis. Life and work meet every single day. For example, many of us have heard the phrase "mommy track," or more rarely, "daddy track," used to describe people who are trying hard to balance work and family life, often to the detriment of their career success. This pejorative trivialization of caregiving, one of the most important roles a human being can undertake, is direct evidence that we need to change our mind-sets about the role of life as it relates to work.

I love when people learn that we allow newborns to be brought into work every day—not as a daycare option but rather to be with their parent. As much as people are intrigued by this possibility, I often hear the question, "Aren't you afraid of the loss of productivity?"

My response is always, "Compared to what?"

How much do worry, anxiety, and scheduling mayhem rob a parent of their productivity? How much productivity is "lost" when a parent must dash out the office when the daycare calls with an incident? And how much do we gain—as individuals and a community—when we see a smile, hear a giggle, or get the chance to witness a baby's very first steps?

As a leader I want to encourage people bringing their vulnerability and full lives to work, yes. But don't forget—aspiration is a part of authenticity too. There will always be a part of work that is "Fake it till you make it." I think that's absolutely fine. We should always be striving for betterment, self-improvement, and personal transformation. Where we go wrong is asking different, more insidious questions. *What kind of leader does the world expect me to be? What kind of leader does my boss want me to be? What leaders seem to achieve the greatest financial success and how can I get the same prize they did?* A much more interesting—and useful—question is *What kind of leader do I want to be?* Asking this constantly is yet another way of bringing your whole self to work.

Fighting Fear by Building Trust

I am neither an expert nor a student of such things, but I suspect that our most powerful human fear is the fear of loneliness or abandonment. Different from a desire for alone time, this is the feeling that we are cut off from others and must fend for ourselves against a dangerous world. Perhaps our survival instincts, honed over the millennia, taught us that isolation and abandonment were our greatest life threat. If our community abandoned us in our primitive days, we were left vulnerable to starvation, cold, and attack by wild animals or enemies. The dangers of our present-day world are different, yet abandonment and isolation in our work lives can lead us down the path to unemployment and all the scary consequences that implies. If career survival is first and foremost on our minds, fear rules our days, and we behave like our primal selves, not our evolved selves.

What is most frightening about this emotion is that we can feel such fearful loneliness even when we are surrounded by others. Obviously, there is much more going on here than simply the absence of others. Perhaps its basis is the absence of *relationships* with others. But how does anyone really build a relationship with another human being?

Our belief at Menlo is that relationships can be built only by spending time together. Many forward-thinking organizations have similarly concluded that positive interteam relationships are crucial to organizational success and spend time on relationship-building events such as company picnics, ropes courses, game nights, Lunch and Learns, and shared mealtimes.

We do these kinds of activities as well. But our best team-building exercise is that *we actually work together.*

Teamwork is a necessary component of authentic leadership. We cannot authentically lead others with whom we have no relationship and there is no better formula for building relationships than spending time together.

James and I can help the situation immensely by not creating a dog-eat-dog, fear-based environment. If we keep fear at bay, people will feel psychologically safe at work. When they feel safe over time, trust has the chance to develop and true collaboration can occur. If these components roll along for long enough, then we can get high-performing teams, the kind that produce human energy and innovative solutions for difficult problems.

If we encourage people to build relationships in a safe environment where they feel valued, not threatened, the masks can start to come off. We can start to see each other as loving, caring, complicated people rather than simply coworkers, staff, employees, or, worse, resources on an org chart.

If you came to observe Menlonians for a while, you'd think we were obsessed with this whole working together thing. Our office opens around 8 a.m. and closes around 6 p.m. We are an in-person company that provides no electronic tether lines to work outside the office. Thus, we all work together all day long, five days a week. We know this is very controversial in some workplace revolution circles, but we believe you lose something important when you are not together.

We do also find a way to integrate remote team members, even if it isn't the norm for us. We are hypervigilant about avoiding the isolation and loneliness described above, and making sure "out of sight, out of mind" does not take root in our culture. For example, each time we send out a team email inviting people out to drinks on a Friday evening to celebrate closing a deal, we think about our traveling team members and how they can be included in the celebration.

We hire and train specifically for togetherness and the ability to build relationships. All initial interviews are group interviews. At your first interview with our company, we pair you with another candidate to work on a problem set and tell you that your mission is to make your pair partner look good and try to help them get a second interview.

Once you're in at Menlo, you work closely with people across the company every single day. Our daily standup meeting includes our whole team. Whoever is in the room at the time (including visitors, dogs, babies, kids) come to standup to discuss what they are working on, where they need help, and any other information they'd like to share. We include our remote team members virtually via FaceTime and send out highlighted notes immediately after our standup so those traveling to client sites are kept in the loop of daily conversations.

Above all—and what most visitors to our company notice first— is that we work in pairs. Two people work together on any given task. We even use electronics cleverly (screen sharing, video cameras, and audio pucks) to pair with our remote team members. This is dynamic: the specific pairings never last more than a week. There is a decided strategy to get everyone to pair with everyone else at some point. With this system, you can't help but learn something about people you work alongside—their style, their experience, their strengths, and even weaknesses. Some of it may be quite personal, though it doesn't have to be.

When we communicate with each other inside the company, we don't use electronics, but rather what we lovingly call High-Speed

Voice Technology—we talk to one another in real time, face-to-face. This system encourages eye contact and proximity. Because of this we ban ear buds and headphones, as we want people to be available to one another.

We didn't adopt these practices because we distrust our team members and want layers of oversight. Rather, we think this environment makes it easier for people to be their authentic selves—and difficult for them to hide behind a version of whom they "think" people want to see.

This work style requires authentic leadership to be successful. In our paired environment, you can start to practice by leading just one other person to embrace an idea you have. By switching pairs frequently, you learn that different people have different styles of influence that work for them. Some need you to inspire them. Others need cold, hard logic. Some need to try something first and learn, while others just want to be taught and then try. Above all, you need leaders to keep the trains running on time, encouraging this practice and bringing their own best and most authentic selves to work as example and proof of how it all works.

One more thing: when I describe this "high relationship" environment, our myriad visitors rush to the defense of the introverts who compose most of the software industry. They assume this setup could never work for them. Our evidence suggests exactly the opposite: we have a couple of strong extroverts on the team, but most of our team members are introverts (including my cofounder) or ambiverts like me. What I've learned through almost twenty years of observation is that introverts don't need sensory deprivation and isolation to thrive as much as safer, deeper relationships. They get that in our space. Our environment isn't social hour and chitchat. It's hard work done *together*, in a space where people feel safe and encouraged to be their true selves.

Reflected Best Self

One of the best things about bringing our authentic selves to work is that by doing so, we can grow and help one another turn vulnerabilities into strengths.

The mask exercise we learned from Ele's Place requires that we first look at our own inside masks and be honest with our harshest critic: ourselves. Most of us, when looking hard at ourselves, will focus on the negative rather than the positive. We will wallow in self-doubt and convince ourselves that the worst thing we could do is reveal the inside of our leadership mask to the world when we don't even enjoy looking at it ourselves. We're also bad at identifying our natural gifts and talents—those things that make us special leaders, leaders worth following. We don't focus on what comes easy to us, instead dwelling on what's difficult or "bad."

But what if we could team with others to discover the traits that are the very *best* parts of our inside mask? What would happen if just for a day we quieted our inner negative voice and listened only to the positive, encouraging voice that keeps saying, "I know this is hard, but you are doing so well. Keep it up. Let me tell you how many things you are doing right . . . "

The academics at the University of Michigan Ross Business School's Center for Positive Organizations shared with us a useful exercise, the Reflected Best Self Exercise, to practice aspirational authenticity. It's simple: you enlist a set of trusted colleagues and friends to write stories about when you were at your best. These can be personal, private stories about when you were the best friend you could be, or stories of things you did at work that brought out the best in someone else. Once you receive and process the stories (be sure to take some time to just revel in them), you look for words and thoughts that are in common across the stories. You then create a "best-self portrait." Warning: we have used this several times at Menlo, and when you receive the feedback from these friends and colleagues, make sure to have a box of tissues nearby. You may be shocked to learn what an amazing person you are. There is in fact a physiological response we have when we receive this kind of feedback; the Ross academics have done research that shows our immune responses increase in saliva tests, for example. It's no wonder we are stressed most of the time, considering how little positive appreciative feedback we get during a regular workday.

Kealy is one of the Menlonians who has participated in this exercise. As she said, "The stories I received from people were invaluable."

Here is her portrait:

Organized • Helper • Kind • Attentive to Detail • Fun • Teacher • Caring • Hard Worker • Bridge • Compassionate • Accepting • Mentor • Understanding • Goofy • Generous Heart • Committed

Can you imagine how powerful it is to have this kind of self-portrait? I encourage you to do a similar exercise to get to know what your authentic superpowers are—to understand what really works for you as a leader, and to reflect and build on those skills instead of passively accepting them and focusing only on your deficiencies, real or imagined.

If You Thought This Step Was Hard . . .

We can't climb straight up the leadership mountain. It will never be that easy. We must use the equivalent of switchbacks to weave our way up. If we get to authenticity on a regular basis (rest assured you'll never get there and stay there), and we start to feel appreciated and honored for the person and leader we really are, then we are ready for the more difficult next part of the climb.

CHAPTER 2

Humble

Build me a son, O Lord, who will be strong enough to know when he is weak, and brave enough to face himself when he is afraid, one who will be proud and unbending in honest defeat, and humble and gentle in victory.

—General Douglas MacArthur

I ARRIVED AT WORK EARLY ONE MORNING AND WAS GREETED BY Tracy B., one of our senior leaders who asked if I had a minute. We pulled up chairs to a table in our training area.

"Are you okay?" she asked me.

The truth is, I wasn't. I had tossed and turned the night before about my less-than-stellar interaction with two of our Quality

Advocates, Tracy and Matt S., the previous afternoon. Now Tracy was doing exactly what I taught her and others on the team to do when a team member is misbehaving—she was calling me on it, speaking truth to power.

"This is about yesterday, isn't it?" I replied.

"Yeah. What you said seemed out of character, so I just wanted to make sure everything is okay."

Sigh. It was time for another trip up humble mountain for me, this time with Tracy by my side.

Let me tell my side of the story . . .

One of my favorite pet projects within Menlo is an iPhone app we developed called Proulx (named for the cofounder of Intuit, Tom Proulx). The app, which is for internal use only, consists of a dashboard that provides a real-time view of Menlo's receivables. I use it to get instant insight into any cash flow challenges that might be on the horizon; in one display, I can see all the outstanding invoices to clients that have not yet been paid. Those that are troubling (invoices that should have been paid by now but haven't) are highlighted in red. Based on my years of leading Menlo, I know that unhappy clients often stop paying their bills in a timely fashion, so red receivables can be the proverbial canary in the client-relationship coal mine.

Internal projects at Menlo are often problematic; it's the classic situation of the shoemaker's kids not having any shoes. We are far more profitable if we focus the talented resources of our team on paying clients rather than our own efforts. As a hedge, we make the internal development efforts slightly more intriguing for our team, giving them opportunities to learn new technologies, run process or architecture experiments, or simply invest in trying out new people off-the-clock of client projects. We intentionally made Proulx a more complex project in order to experiment with a variety of approaches.

For a quick technical background (I am, after all, still a software engineer at heart): The Proulx system extracts data regularly from our Quickbooks accounting system using the Microsoft language C#, then prepares and formats the data for upload to the Amazon Cloud using COBOL.* Once uploaded, the data are organized on the Amazon Web Services cloud servers for download using the Python language and then ultimately displayed with the app on my iPhone using the latest language from Apple called Swift. I introduce all this stuff to say this little app that seems so simple in concept has a lot of moving parts. I love this app, and I proudly show it off when clients ask what we do at Menlo.

The extra complexity of the project wasn't necessary, but we had other intentions for the team doing the work. This has led to a couple of challenges with the project that I wish weren't there. The app doesn't always update properly, and sometimes I am looking at old data or no data. Since this is a learning project for us when we have extra talent available, I shouldn't be surprised when it doesn't work right. Right?

Well, this particular week, the team was tasked with fixing the update problems I was seeing. During testing, the day before my

---

* Yup, you read that right. Most people don't realize that half of big business systems today still run in 1960s vintage COBOL. We didn't want our team intimidated by paying projects that might include COBOL, so we used this project to give our modern developers exposure to an important legacy language.

morning meeting with Tracy, she and Matt reported results to me. Since I was the primary sponsor of the project, they wanted to know some of my expectations for the improvements being made. I told them I was disappointed that the app often didn't have the most up-to-date data. I asked Matt how often and on what schedule the data were pulled from our QuickBooks server.

"I don't know," Matt replied.

To say I was disappointed with Matt's response was an understatement. I think my reply was pretty straightforward, along the lines of, "Well, Matt, as one of the Quality Advocates on a project, I would expect you to know how the system was architected and what the expected behaviors are and be able to tell me when I ask. This is exactly what our clients expect, so why shouldn't I expect the same as the sponsor of this project?" I'll bet I even used my best boss voice and facial expressions too.

Tracy and Matt stopped talking and looked at each other. Then Matt said "Okay," and he and Tracy walked back to their workstation to continue their work. I knew right away I hadn't handled that very well.

There are a few important posters on the walls and pillars of Menlo. One of the biggest posters—and a catchphrase of our culture—reads "It's OK to Say I Don't Know." Yet I had castigated Matt for saying "I don't know"—right underneath that poster, in fact. Yikes.

That evening I thought about the moment and reflected on how I could have done better. It was an internal learning project, after all, and what I was modeling for these team members was how to be a poor leader to one of the newer members of the team. I had work to do to repair this relationship and admit my mistake.

Before I even had a chance to say anything to Matt and Tracy the next morning, Tracy pulled me aside to see if I was OK, recognizing the behavior wasn't normal for me or Menlo. Just as Tracy and I started the conversation, Matt walked in the front door for work that day. I motioned him over to join us.

As he sat down, I immediately told him, "Matt, yesterday when you and Tracy approached me about Proulx, I didn't handle that conversation very well. And I just want to say I'm sorry."

Without missing a beat, and with total sincerity, Matt replied, "I forgive you."

You can learn humility from anyone, at any moment. Matt barely knew me, as he had only joined the team a few months before. Yet he had already internalized our values so well that he was able to accept an apology from the CEO with far more humility than I had shown to him the day before. I grew a little that day, thanks to Matt and Tracy.

Humble is a challenging word in the context of business. Humble may be seen as the opposite of what you should be seeking. After all, if our business is "humble," won't our competition walk all over us? If any one of us is "humble," won't we be overlooked for the next promotion or bonus in favor of others who are doing a better job of staying in the limelight and promoting themselves, especially when the boss is in eyeshot?

For me, being humble doesn't mean being a doormat. Being humble means *considering others*. As leaders, we can and should support our employees and team members, making sure they are taken care of first, as Simon Sinek memorably relayed in *Leaders Eat Last*, not pushing to the front of a line because we think we've "earned it" by virtue of an arbitrary title.

Humility acknowledges that all work is noble, even the mundane. If I truly believe all work is vital to the company's success, I shouldn't be reticent to put in effort on tasks that some would consider below my pay grade. It's why you'll see me cleaning up after client lunches on occasion. If this is a behavior I want to see in the organization, I'd better be willing to follow through on it myself, not just expect it from others. And while I do need reminders from time to time (thanks, Tracy and Matt), I think it's important for a leader to show humility consistently.

Lessons from *The Giving Tree*

The Giving Tree by Shel Silverstein is one of the saddest books a parent can read to their child. In fact, I'd argue it is not a book for children but for parents, because it's about unconditional love, about turning your life over to another and doing so with delight, patience, and perseverance. The Giving Tree continually gives pieces of itself away to someone else who is less patient, less wise, less experienced, and more ambitious, someone who will suffer setbacks and disappointments. Eventually the tree becomes a stump that's good only for sitting and resting. And it does this all with joy.

This is humility in action—putting others first without expectation of rewards. Are we ready to lead like this? Am I? This approach is contrary to what most of us have witnessed in our work.

We all have work to do as employees or executives. It is the responsibility and role we trained for, went to college for, or learned through on-the-job training. Our competence at this work defines our standing in our workplace. If we are new to our profession, we start at a lower rank and as we demonstrate proficiency, we are recognized for that increased value through raises and promotions. This cycle composes the daily work of our employment.

Leadership is different. Leaders are faced with the ambiguity of guiding others, considering the need of short-term results against the long-term benefits of growing the people around you. If you've grown insanely competent at your work, and you are now being asked to increase the competence of others so that one day they can do your work at least as well as you do, you can either be expedient and do it yourself or teach. Leaders choose to teach. And teaching is an inherently humble act—focusing first and foremost on the development of others.

To do this, we always need to remember that those people we work with—our employees, customers, vendors—are human beings first, not objects or a means to an end. This is harder than it should be.

One person who really figured this out is my great friend and mentor, Bob Chapman, CEO of Barry-Wehmiller and author of *Everybody Matters: The Extraordinary Power of Caring for Your People Like Family*. Bob, who runs a billion-dollar manufacturing company, encourages us to remember that employees are someone's son or daughter. And whether you're a parent or a son or daughter yourself (everyone is one of these!), consider how you would want to see people treated at work. This is the lens through which Barry-Wehmiller operates: humans first, with no one human better than another one, and with everyone caring for the whole as if they are one big family. This is humility in action.

Humility requires a great deal of a very special kind of strength. Yet not the kind of strength—overpowering, authoritative—many think is the hallmark of good business leadership. Remember the tremendous power of putting others first and not holding yourself above those around you, and your life will be filled with the kind of rich rewards that no price tag can measure. And humble strength allows us to bring something else to work that most don't expect would be a value in the world of business.

CHAPTER 3

Loving

Only the weak are cruel. Gentleness can only be expected from the strong.

—Leo Buscaglia, from his book *Love*

IF THERE IS A CORE TENET UPON WHICH I WOULD BUILD MY LEAD-
ership life, and in doing so inspire those I led, it is this: love wins every time. Particularly if the victory you seek is different from busyness and obedience. If you want engagement, if you want your team to lead even when you are not there, then only love will work. Not fear, not intimidation, not bullying or bravado, and not by being the smartest guy in the room.

In the context of leadership, it may be helpful to think of love as the absence of its opposites. To be a loving leader means to not be cruel. Or mean. Or harsh. Or impatient. Or unkind. Or uncaring. Or vindictive. Or sarcastic. Or hurtful. I never want our leaders to be any of those things. I don't want to be any of those things either.

In thinking about loving leadership, I am reminded of the famous First Corinthians passage. What it says about love in general, it could also say about the love that leaders should show for those they lead:

"Love is patient, love is kind. It does not envy, it does not boast, it is not proud. It does not dishonor others, it is not self-seeking, it is not easily angered, it keeps no record of wrongs. Love does not delight in evil but rejoices with the truth. It always protects, always trusts, always hopes, always perseveres."

Loving leadership really brings out the best in people, and it enables you to share your best, most effective self with others you interact with.

Leadership Is Patient

Our greatest impulse as bosses and managers is expediency in the name of efficiency. Just think of how often we will do something for short-term results and not worry about the long-term consequences. Later we will lament that we don't have the right people, they aren't working hard enough, they don't seem to have the skills needed, or "they" just don't understand the highest priorities as well as "we" do.

In fact, the us-versus-them mind-set is a very damaging aspect of most leadership teams. If only *they* cared as much as *we* do. But of course *they* don't, because *they* are not *us*.

Our moments of impatience can have effects that last a lifetime. My mom demonstrated throughout my life the best example of unconditional love I likely will ever experience. However, I remember one time, when I was in fourth grade, I needed help with homework and Mom was likely rushed, or having a bad day, and very uncharacteristically criticized my penmanship. I don't think I have written in cursive since that day, presuming that if Mom didn't think I could do it, I just couldn't. (It would break her heart to read this today, some fifty years later.)

How many times do we do something similar as leaders, say something without thinking because we are in a hurry and not fully present, and therefore more liable to be dismissive or even cruel? Do we assume that everyone recovers from our hurtful words? What if they don't? What effect does this absence of patience, over time, have on the growth and development of the people around us?

One of our longtime team members had such a moment with our team a few years ago. When a newer team member rose from her seat at a project kickoff meeting to take the whiteboard and offer her thoughts, he motioned her down with his hand and said, "I got this." I get it; he thought he was more qualified based on his years of experience with Menlo and that project. However, that public dressing down of a team member sent a shockwave through the team.

As we weren't as polished then at giving constructive feedback to him, this event, in combination with other moments that distanced him from the team, eventually led to his leaving the company. We lost a team member due to his lack of loving care for a new team member who needed a mentor more than a dressing down. I'd say this was a love deficiency in every way. He could have been a better leader in that moment, and, quite frankly, I could have been too.

Leadership Is Kind (and Kindness Is Free)

You've probably come across that famous Leo Durocher quote about sports: "Nice guys finish last."

There are so many sports metaphors that work their way into the business lexicon that it would seem business and sports are quite the same. I disagree, and I *love* sports.

When we apply the Durocher quote to business, we imply that to finish in first place, kindness needs to take a backseat to the aggressive pursuit of winning. The trouble is, what does a first-place finish in business even mean? In sports it is clear—one team loses and another wins. In business, however, it's not always so cut-and-dried.

Kindness may be the most valuable currency a leader has. Kindness does not mean "looking the other way." Rather, kindness means caring, the deepest kind of caring. The caring that might mean a tough conversation or a firing.

Recently I met a gentleman named Rick K. who approached me, introduced himself, and asked me if I remembered him. I didn't.

"I worked for you back in the eighties," he said.

I was still having trouble conjuring the memory.

"You fired me."

It all came flooding back in an instant. I had hired this young man right out of school, a bright young engineer with loads of promise. The problem I witnessed firsthand was that work wasn't necessarily on his list of priorities. He had a habit of chatting up the company receptionist every day just outside of my office. His assignments lagged, and work just didn't seem to matter to him. We were a small company and every little piece of effort mattered, a lot. But not to him.

Even with coaching, he didn't get it, so I let him go. It may have been the very first firing of my management career. And now, decades later, I was eye to eye with him.

"I just have to tell you your talk with me that day has lasted a lifetime. I was never the same since," he continued.

Oh. How much damage had I done? I'm sure I wasn't very good at this sort of thing back then. I should ask his forgiveness, I thought, and reflected on how I learned to be a better leader since then. I held my breath as he finished his story.

"You coached me about what was important at work. How hard work pays off and being self-aware of bad behavior is so vital to my career. Those words and the way you delivered them changed my life, and I have excelled ever since. I just wanted to say thank you."

Wow. That was unexpected.

Kindness may not always be easy when we are in these tough moments. Leaders are human too. We are under pressure to deliver results, get our work done, take care of our family, pay our bills, pursue our dreams, and work through the overall challenges of life, health, and love and other emotions. Yet we must remember that in the most important moments of leadership when a hard message is needed, that message can be delivered with kindness, caring, love, and compassion.

At every point in our dealings with others, we can be harsh or kind. Both approaches are free, but one comes at a high cost. Don't ever forget this. I have worked for some unkind bosses in my lifetime and my greatest delight was in quitting, leaving them behind and never looking back. Their lack of kindness was instructive to my future style, as I learned what kind of leader I *didn't* want to be.

When coaching team members, I ask them to act toward each other as if they were going to spend an eternity in heaven together. Regardless of your beliefs, it's a good mental model for every conversation.

Leadership Does Not Envy

I had an abundantly rich upbringing of love and learning. Material stuff? Not so much. Never hurting, mind you, but I suspect those wonderful camping trips that provided me with such amazing memories of my childhood were also the only vacations my parents could afford at the time. I received great memories at a very low price. I will be forever indebted to my parents for those memories and the love they gave my brothers and me.

I wanted, and was able, to give and receive the love my parents so lavishly showered on my brothers and me. The love in my family was and is palpable, and that is a blessing beyond measure.

Can you hear the "but" in everything above? But I still wanted. Stuff. Things. Status. A nice house, fun car, memorable vacation, the latest shiny Apple gadget. I envied others and their possessions and trappings of success.

My envy came to a head earlier in my career. I looked at those above me on the ladder. They drove nicer cars, threw parties at their much nicer homes, and their kids went to amazing and expensive schools. They lived in nicer neighborhoods, the neighborhoods whose names everyone knew: Ann Arbor's Burns Park, Barton Hills, and the West Side come to mind. They had better titles than I and bigger offices and more authority. If I was a manager, they were directors. If I was a director, they were VPs. Ugh.

I could always feel my impatience in these envious moments. How long did I have to wait before all of that could be mine?

Then it was. I became the Senior VP of R&D at Interface after we were acquired by a high-flying Redwood City, California, company in 1999. Nobody was bigger than I was in Ann Arbor. I was the boss. And I was miserable. I couldn't sleep at night. I tossed and turned at the politics, the harshness, the ruthlessness, and the ambition as we all pursued higher and higher stock prices such that our options were worth millions. At the height of the internet bubble my little spreadsheet told me my Interface Systems stock options were worth nearly $4 million. Surely, that would be enough, right? I recall one financial adviser at the time encouraging me to begin converting these high-risk shares for something a little more secure. Why? I asked him. Everyone else is making so much in this crazy time, so why not me? Yes, Interface stock is trading at $80 a share, yes we are the No. 1 public company in Michigan in terms of stock growth, but we are a skyrocketing high-tech firm and the pundits are saying we are heading to $150 a share. My worth will climb to $7 million. I wouldn't want to miss out on that, would I? Besides, I am in control of the destiny of this stock. Its worth is growing like this because of me, right?

I had the world by the tail and all my ambitious dreams were coming true.

Then it *all* disappeared, in an instant. The bubble burst and I lost it all: stock, company, job, title, paycheck, team, authority, parking spot, office, desk, computer. I applied for unemployment. College loans were what got and kept my then-college-aged daughters fed and in school.

My life is now rich beyond measure. My wife and I still live in the same humble home, the one filled with the joyful memories of raising our girls, and now filled with the noise of the most beautiful, funny, lovable granddaughters the world has ever seen. I sleep well at night. I am as much in control of my work destiny as one can imagine. The company that I started with my partners fulfills me beyond my wildest dreams, though success looks different from what I thought it should look like back at Interface.

I make good money now, but nothing like what I hear about CEOs at other companies making. I no longer envy their lavish lifestyles and offices. I sit at a five-foot table out in the room with everyone else. You'd never be able to pick out the CEO "office" from that of the rest of the team. I like that: it takes envy out of the equation.

Leading from a place of acceptance and gratitude for what you have, rather than from out-of-control envy, is always more effective. It allows you to focus on what really matters, not play a game you can't win anyway. I encourage you to confront your own envy, and focus on loving what you have, not what you think you want.

Leadership Is Not Proud

One of the most culturally dangerous words at Menlo is "I." As described earlier, most of our work is done in pairs. The work is communally shared such that the work done by a pair one week is continued by another pair the next week, with one of the two people from the previous week's pair continuing for the second week with their new partner. This workforce "square dance" cycle repeats weekly on projects that last months or years.

Can you imagine how hard it would be in our environment to say, "I did this" or "That is my work"? It is virtually always "our work together."

This simple construct likely betrays many management gurus' fundamental premises of building a high-performance team. There is a fallacy that bringing together individual high performers is the most expedient route to a great team. Consider all the business axioms around "best and brightest" and "A players."

At Menlo, we prefer hiring the kids who got As in kindergarten more so than at MIT. This thinking certainly confounds the traditional individual performance appraisal processes. Our tour guests invariably ask how we measure *individual* performance in such an environment. Our answer confounds them even more: we couldn't care less about individual performance, especially when it comes at the expense of the team. As you might imagine, brains contort with the illogic of this statement. Yet this is exactly what leadership looks like!

If you desire to run your company with loads of leaders and few, if any, bosses, you better take a hard look at with how much emphasis you place "I" and "me" in front of "we" and "us."

Let's take this up a notch and remind you of the moments in your career where this happened to you. You and your peers slaved away on a project for months, jettisoning time with family, delaying vacations, coming home late, and missing dinners. Now imagine if, when the delivery was made, someone up the chain of command talked about how "I led the team that did this." Uh-huh. Sure.

This kind of prideful boasting doesn't happen all that often in reality. Most bosses are self-aware enough to make sure they credit the team with the effort and the accomplishment. But when it comes to bonus time, who gets the biggest bonus and the most stock options?

The boss didn't have to boast, didn't have to say, "I did this." Every reward system in the corporation says it for them: *you* are important, so we give *you* a big office, a big bonus, a special parking place. I worked at one company where you could literally measure your status with a tape measure. How high were your cube walls? How many square feet of office? How big is your window? Door? Or no door? The bigwigs got to park in the indoor heated parking lot (a big deal in Ann Arbor in the winter months).

I believe one of the most important moves we made in the

earliest days of Menlo was to ensure our profit-sharing bonuses were *equal* among team members. Not equal in percentage of pay, but equal in terms of dollar amount. This makes it very clear that every person contributes to the company. The smartest engineer who created the cleverest algorithm does not matter more to our success than the person who answered the phone pleasantly and helped introduce us to our next million-dollar client. The truth is no one in any company knows for sure what magic moments or mundane efforts lead to success—and we should focus on and find pride in team accomplishments first.

Leadership Does Not Dishonor Others

In our political arena, we see candidates get elected because they made their opponent look as bad as possible. When organizations become political, this happens too: gossip, innuendo, backstabbing, withholding information or assistance for personal gain or promotion.

There is an infamous and sad tale of one high-flying tech firm whose ambitious young leaders would boastfully declare to their own teams that they were withholding information from their bosses. The intent was to make their bosses look bad to the next level up in the hope that they would get sacked, paving a way for the junior bosses to be promoted in their stead. Yikes! I wonder in that environment how well their direct reports were imprinting the lessons of this horrible behavior.

Many leadership and personal development courses encourage

you to write your own obituary. I'd like to ensure that my grave-stone does not read: "Here Lies Richard Sheridan. He Stepped on Everyone He Could to Get Here."

Let me say it simply: honor others. It's a critical component of leadership.

One of my favorite people on the planet is Arnetha H., a de-lightfully proud mom and hardworking custodian at The Univer-sity of Michigan. I see Arnetha nearly every morning when I go to write at the Michigan Union on State Street. Among her daily re-sponsibilities is keeping the Michigan Union reading room in tip-top shape. It occurred to me to thank her for her diligent efforts back in 2013 while writing *Joy, Inc.* We have been great friends ever since, and I often begin my writing days with a hug from Arnetha. Her beautiful smile and bright eyes start my day with joy. She is always interested in me and what I am doing, and we delight in catching up on each other's families.

How many Arnethas are there in our world, those people who selflessly and tirelessly make the world a better place for everyone? Remember to honor them and the myriad others who help us in ways large and small. Like offering kindness, this kind of honoring is free.

Leaders often fail to honor people, since "they're just doing their job." But consider how much a "thank you" could do to con-tinue to encourage good work. We will never know the complete stories of the people who work for us and around us. We have no idea what their struggles are at home, or what other demons they may be carrying with them each day.

Go thank someone for something you see them doing, and yes, even if it is "their job." Thank someone in your organization; thank someone you interact with daily but may never have thought to acknowledge with gratitude before. This kind of simple leadership move can make a huge difference in the lives of the people around you.

Leadership Is Not Self-seeking

Many young leaders in our community ask me out for coffee and advice. I remember how other leaders have shared their wisdom with me and I am forever grateful for every minute they've shared, so I try to pay it back in-kind by making myself as available as I possibly can. My time sheets list this time as either "mentoring" or "community networking." I can spend as much as 25 percent of my workweek on these activities. I enjoy getting to know people, their life stories, and I try to share some wisdom I've gained along the way.

Invariably, these mentoring discussions turn to the topic of ambition, and perhaps even a bit of envy, like I've described earlier. The committed young leaders I meet with wonder how they can get on a leadership and promotion track. I'm guessing they see something in me they like or perhaps a bit of what I've accomplished, and they want encouragement on how to achieve similar results for themselves.

In my employment history, my bosses found me, promoted me, and put me in positions of leadership. Much of what I had to learn was done in on-the-job training and loads of trial and error. I screwed up nearly as often as I succeeded. The key lesson I've learned, though, is to not seek the position or the authority. Just be a leader. You can lead from anywhere. If you get good enough at it, and aren't doing it for your own self-seeking reasons, the right things will happen. A promotion itself won't make you a leader.

I believe some of my early leadership development experience came from coaching my daughters' T-ball teams. Teaching five-year-olds just to run around the bases in the right sequence and laughing while doing it produced some tremendous leadership growth moments. If you don't believe me, consider this for two of the T-ball coaches who paired together to lead those teams: me, programmer then, now CEO of Menlo, and Phil Hanlon, U-M math professor then, now president of Dartmouth, after a successful career as provost at the University of Michigan. Random? Maybe. But I know it was a great leadership experience for me, in an unexpected and unsought situation.

And be a little patient. I know youth and patience don't always go well together, and if you add a big scoop of ambition, a potentially toxic mix can result. In the case of leadership, the wisdom of years and experience are invaluable. No MBA, no single book, no promotion can prepare you for the challenging dynamics of leadership. Throw in a title, and hierarchical authority on top of inexperience, and you may find yourself leading in the worst way possible: without anyone following.

Leadership Is Not Easily Angered

I get angry. Ask my wife. Ask my daughters. Ask my cofounder and many Menlonians. I don't like it when I get angry, and it is rare. I believe the Menlonians would agree that I am not *easily* angered. In fact, I think the team would sometimes like to see it more often.

I'm more likely to get angry when I am stressed, overtired, or as my wife, Carol, knows, when I am hungry.

It's embarrassing sometimes. The anger doesn't feel like me and it's not what I aspire to. Sometimes my passion gets the best of me. My anger can flow when my expectations are high and the results aren't, particularly from people I am counting on.

I am pretty sure that nothing good ever came from these moments, except perhaps a good apology later. I would even say I was angry when Matt S. told me "I don't know" when I asked him about the Proulx outages. I didn't lash out or anything, I'm pretty sure I didn't even raise my voice, but I was nowhere near my best self. A loud voice does not always accompany anger.

Learning to control your emotions is likely one of the most fundamentals skills of leadership. My good friend Paul Saginaw, cofounder of Zingerman's, has an excellent phrase to use during these leadership moments: "When furious, get curious."

I love that for two reasons. First, it channels your anger in a positive direction. The angrier you are, the more curious you should be about why you're reacting that way. Consider how powerful it is to redirect your energy in this manner. Second, this implies that you likely don't have the full picture of any situation. You might have the story only in your own head. VitalSmarts, the leadership training organization whose founders and authors brought us the famous books *Crucial Conversations* and *Influencer,* calls on us to use this moment to "master your stories." I like the idea of being a master of my emotions.

I need to get better at this, and I will be a better leader if I do. That is true for all of us. If our teams never know whether Dr. Jekyll or Mr. Hyde is walking in the door today, how likely are they to approach us with the pressing problems of the day and ask for help?

Leadership Does Not Keep a Record of Wrongs

I have a bad memory when it comes to things that have gone wrong. Perhaps it is wishful thinking on my part: If I forget what you did wrong, will you please forget what I did wrong?

Keeping a mental list of wrongs is one of the most insidious leadership errors. If you are the leader who ruminates on everything that went wrong, or everyone who did you wrong, you will be paralyzed, unable to move forward. No one will follow you for fear of moving from the inner circle to the outer circle and staying there forever. If you are thinking, *But don't we need to keep this list for their annual performance review?* No! If something happens you don't like, go have the conversation and move on. If the conversation happens again and again, dig deeper with the employee—ask them if they are OK or if there's a reason they think this mistake keeps happening. If the repeated occurrence threatens their employment, tell them that.

A leader's job is not to keep a list of wrongs and spring it on the staff at their annual performance review. I can hear compliance people and legal teams assuring me that a written list of wrongs is very important if you are going to let someone go. I will tell you what is more important: *treating people with dignity and respect.* When I think of the people in my career who struggled the most with personal growth and leadership growth, it is often those who can't let go of some injustice that happened, sometimes years before.

The worst form of this in the corporate world is the dreaded "blackball" list of former employees, especially the list of those who quit and are told they will never work at the company again because of their disloyalty.

We've never had that policy at Menlo. Some employees who have left us we wouldn't necessarily want back, but we'd still give even them a second chance. Maybe they've changed. Maybe we've changed.

Ian F. is our best example that people can and do change. He has left Menlo three times, and each time he returned as a better Ian. We doubted this was even possible. The first time he resigned we were relieved, because he was within a couple of weeks of being fired. His challenging nature was on the hairy edge of insubordination. When he called a couple of years later and asked whether we'd consider having him back, we told him we weren't sure. We came up with an experiment; he would have to go through our standard three-week trial period again to see if he was a right fit for the team again. He understood completely and agreed. He passed with flying colors.

Within weeks, it was clear to me we inherited a very different Ian. I asked him what happened to him to make for such a dramatic change. He told me that when he left, he just didn't believe in the Menlo approach to software development. He also wasn't happy that we wouldn't listen to the big changes he thought we should make in the company. But with his new employer, he started seeing all the problems James and I continually lamented were out there in the real world. Each time Ian flexed his leadership muscles in his new job, he started pushing his new employer to the Menlo way of doing things, and business improved.

"Rich, do you know how hard it is to build Menlo?" he asked me.

"I kind of do, Ian," I replied with a wink and a smile.

Ian told me how he woke up one day and wondered why he was working so hard to rebuild Menlo when he could possibly go back to work at Menlo. Upon his return Ian quickly became one of our most revered leaders. He held others accountable to the culture we created but he did so in such a loving, caring way. If he was telling you that you were screwing up, he did so with *you* in mind. He had high expectations for those around him and if they fell short, he helped them succeed by being the best teacher he could be.

Within a few years, entrepreneurial longing beckoned and Ian joined a start-up founded by another former Menlonian. When his work there was done, he joined us again. No three-week trial this time, and now his entrepreneurial lessons again improved his leadership style as he now had an appreciation for the "business" of Menlo, not just the technical work.

The third time Ian left, he did so because he received a monetary offer he couldn't refuse. On leaving, he told me that he wanted to bring even more lessons back to Menlo the next time. I believed him. He is back again, and the team is thrilled. Our company is better for having taken Ian back each time, and had we held on to a grudge that he left us in the first place, we would not have benefited from having a smarter, gentler, more giving leader with us at those points in our journey and his.

Leadership Does Not Delight in Evil but Rejoices in the Truth

As a Michigander, I was fascinated by *American Icon: Alan Mulally and the Fight to Save Ford Motor Company*, Bryce Hoffman's book about Ford's turnaround as led by CEO Alan Mulally. One of the most memorable stories centers on a Thursday leadership meeting at which Mulally's top leaders were reporting project statuses.

Mulally had been tasked with turning around a company in dire straits. To start, he implemented a color code—every executive had to give a report on his or her division and projects by stating whether it was green (going great), yellow (on the edge), or red (in trouble.) For the first few weeks, when it came time to present an update, every executive responded with "Green, boss," meaning that everything was running smoothly.

Mulally knew he couldn't appropriately lead an organization that was about to lose $7 billion if the only answer every top leader in his organization could give was "All okay, boss, I'm green."

The head of North American Operations, longtime Ford executive Mark Fields, had to order a shutdown of production of the

Ford Edge, due to a production quality issue. He knew he couldn't hide the news and assumed that when he reported "Red, boss" to his CEO at that week's meeting, it would mark his last day at Ford Motor Company. But when he told Mulally he had red on his sheet, Mulally's reaction was to applaud (literally clapping) and thank Mark for telling the truth. He then asked his other team members "How are we going to help Mark?" In that moment, a new day dawned at Ford and likely saved the company.

I know this radical embracing of the truth changed the culture at Ford. I play golf with an eclectic group that includes some Ford folks, including Vic G., who runs the league. One league night in 2016, after having just finished *American Icon,* I asked Vic if he had read the book yet. He hadn't. He didn't need to, he said, because he lived the story.

From my reading I knew that, in 2006, every employee was given a pocket-size One Ford card that outlined the company's mission and values. "Did you take that card seriously?" I asked Vic. Without missing a beat, Vic took out his wallet and showed me his One Ford card.

On a card, small enough to fit in your wallet, headed by the famous blue Ford oval logo, it read:

ONE FORD
ONE TEAM. ONE PLAN. ONE GOAL.
ONE TEAM
People working together as a lean, global enterprise for automotive leadership, as measured by:

*Customer, Employee, Dealer, Investor, Supplier, Union/
Council and Community Satisfaction*

ONE PLAN

Aggressively restructure to operate profitably at the current demand and changing model mix

Accelerate development of new products our customers want and value

Finance our plan and improve our balance sheet

Work together effectively as one team

ONE GOAL*

An exciting viable Ford delivering profitable growth for all

Vic—not a man prone to hyperbole in any way—had been carrying this card with pride for a decade. Think about what that means and how significant an impact Alan Mulally made on the culture in orienting it away from fear and toward truth and teamwork, that an employee would carry that card around every single day. I recently met a woman who was on the Ford team back then, and when I asked about the One Ford card she immediately looked at her purse indicating she also still carried it around—and she doesn't even work there anymore!

I don't believe there is much true evil in the world, and certainly not in most corporations or leadership teams. The reason

---

* Bryce G. Hoffman, *American Icon: Alan Mulally and the Fight to Save Ford Motor Company* (New York: Currency, 2013).

truly bad corporate behavior makes headlines is because it is rare and newsworthy, not because it is common. There is also not as much "rejoicing in the truth" as there needs to be. The stupid quarterly revenue pushes of public corporations and the tomfoolery evident in M&A transactions, where results are inflated just prior to a sale only for the resulting merger to fail shortly after, suggests truth is not handsomely rewarded and getting to it is difficult. Most SEC regulations are focused on various tools to get at the truth, but these tools are still about as crude as the sharp sticks and rocks of our caveman days.

We must consider the role that fear plays in hiding truth and the means we must employ as leaders to get at the truth. More important, we need to figure out our equivalent of Mulally's applause when the truth reveals troubling news.

At Menlo, our open environment, our visual artifacts of work, and posting project status on wallboard displays is a physical attempt to keep the true status of our work out where everyone can see it, every day. Each task's status is coded with a colorful sticky dot. A piece of yarn moves down the board like clockwork every day. Tasks with green dots above the string mean we are on track for that task. Yellow or red dots above the string mean that task is behind. This simple mechanism gives us a peek at schedule performance truth, which is very important to the project-based work that drives the majority of our revenue.

We added one more element to this system to reward truth, which was teaching our project managers to smile (actually smile) and say thank you when delays were reported by the team. We are all human and none of us like to fail or make mistakes. But if we trade this fear-mongering bureaucracy for honoring truth and even rewarding it—facing it head on—we have a brighter future.

Leadership Protects, Always Trusts, Always Hopes, Always Perseveres

If there is a job for leaders this is it: preserving, protecting, defending our teams, our culture, our people, our vision for the future, our values.

We do some weird things at Menlo that get us a lot of attention, and yet we find other amazing companies that have their own version of weirdness in the name of preserve, protect, and defend.

For example, Charlie Kim and Meghan Messenger, co-CEOs of Next Jump Associates, have a "never fire anyone rule." Once you get the vaunted Next Jump jacket from your peers, they commit to preserve, protect, and defend you even if you aren't doing such a great job at that yourself. Your peers take ownership of you as if you were family.

In an interview with David Marquet, author of *Turn the Ship Around*, Charlie shared how Next Jump shifted from a policy of letting go the bottom 10 percent of performers to not firing at all, starting in 2012.

"Once you realize that you are entering into a lifelong relationship, hiring starts to look a lot more like adoption, or dating. Multiple interactions over some time are required before our team would get comfortable with a prospective hire. Every hiring manager started hiring more carefully, something I'd been advocating for but couldn't make happen in every manager. Without further direction, they started treating hiring like adoption: once we take someone into our family, they're here for life. When things don't work, they're responsible for training them, helping them. Training also became much more comprehensive, touching subjects such as character, grit, and integrity in ways we had previously viewed as beyond the scope of company training."*

This idea that hiring is like an adoption, and that once adopted, you are like family, was further reinforced for Charlie and Meghan by Bob Chapman of Barry-Wehmiller (whom I mentioned in the last chapter). Bob and Charlie were talking about Charlie's original practice of "fast firing" to put the employee and the company out of the misery of a bad match. Bob asked Charlie how he would feel if he heard his son was fired from a job. In that moment, Charlie realized that a firing is the equivalent of having someone important in your life telling you "You're no good." If he didn't want that for his son, why would he want that for his team members?

I find it fascinating that for both Bob and Charlie, these journeys of protection and perseverance were not born in times of abundance but in scarcity. Charlie's company was nearly destroyed in the dot-com bust, and Bob's was threatened during the 2008 financial crisis. It is always easy to imagine being a great leader during times

---

* "How would a #NoFirePolicy affect your company? An interview with NextJump CEO Charlie Kim who decided to do just that." https://www.davidmarquet.com/2013/02/02/how-would-a-nofirepolicy-affect-your-company-an-interview-with-nextjump-ceo-charlie-kim-who-decided-to-do-just-that/.

of abundance, but our value as leaders is only put to the test when hard times hit.

When those hard times hit us, we must show love to keep moving forward. And . . . our teams will be looking for us to keep them energized about the future, no matter the present situation.

CHAPTER 4

Optimistic

Between stimulus and response there is a space. In that space is our power to choose our response. In our response lies our growth and our freedom.

—Viktor Frankl

THE YEAR 2015 ENDED AS MENLO'S BEST TO DATE IN OUR fourteen-year history. We rang every business bell you can ring: revenues, profits, profit sharing, cash in the bank, tour and visitors counts, successful projects. We were in that place every business dreams of.

Come 2016 and it all stopped, suddenly and dramatically.

Current projects ended, and new ones weren't showing up to replace them. Potential clients were still inquiring, but they weren't deciding in our favor, or they weren't deciding at all. Fear was running amok in the marketplace too. China was slowing down, the EU was threatened by the Brexit vote, and the Fed was toying dangerously with vacillating stories about interest rates. There were horrible examples of violence in our nation, the presidential election process seemed to enjoy fanning the flames of fear to prove that the other side "just wasn't getting how serious all of our problems were," oil prices were at historic lows, and stock indices jumped all over the place. In short, there was fear, big fear, and businesses just stopped making decisions and were hoarding cash. The lessons of 2009 were still too fresh in everyone's mind.

James and I never wavered. We knew the business would come, and we used the time to work on internal skill building and laying out the vision for the company for the next ten years. We opened the A2 Startup Garage, offering office space to cash-strapped, culture-curious start-ups in the extra 6,000 square feet at the back of our building. We also focused a lot of effort on getting our open-book financial management in full operation.

One day as I stood at my desk, Lisa H., one of our senior leaders, asked me a simple but profound question: "Rich, where does your optimism come from?"

She wasn't just referring to my attitude in that specific moment. She had seen in me a relentless optimism throughout our history, in good times and not so good times. This wasn't an anomaly, but the way I deliberately led the team.

Simon Sinek wrote that, "Leaders are the ones who run head-first into the unknown, they rush toward the danger. They put their own safety aside to protect us or pull us into the future."* Now, we weren't *blindly* rushing into a dangerous unknown with our optimism. We knew we had to try things, run experiments, serious leadership experiments, to prepare ourselves for when things got busy again. And they did, and we were ready. James and I also had to be there to reassure the doubters on our team who wanted very specific answers to very specific questions.

When you follow a leader, sometimes you just want to know that everything is going to be OK. *Justifiable* optimism can go a long way to keeping irrational fear at bay and keeping the focus on the long term.

Optimism Is a Choice

Every important moment in a leader's life comes with an equally important choice: How will we respond to this situation? Will we choose to line up the dominoes in our mind and start them tumbling toward the worst possible outcome or the best? Do we assume others have good intent or not? Do we assume things will go right or wrong?

Optimism is a fundamental choice of leadership.

Choosing optimism is not about choosing sunshine, rainbows, and unicorns. It is about believing in two possibilities with as much

---

* Simon Sinek, *Leaders Eat Last: Why Some Teams Pull Together and Others Don't* (New York: Portfolio, 2017).

73

wisdom as we can muster. The first is good intent on the part of the people around you—your employees, your customers, your community. The second is the belief that if things don't go as well as you expect, you will have set up the conditions such that you will have time to make other choices that can get things back on track.

In Edward de Bono's famous book *Six Thinking Hats,* he introduces six different approaches to thinking about any given situation. The White Hat looks at a situation solely through the lens of known and knowable facts, like an emotionless Mr. Spock using data to come to a conclusion. In contrast, the Red Hat represents our emotional response to a situation or idea. He or she asks, "How does it make us feel?" De Bono's Black Hat is often depicted as the hat of the engineer. When we engineers look at an idea or a situation, the Black Hat has us consider "What if something goes wrong, and what if it goes wrong in this way?" This is critical to success. We must consider the possibilities of failure or system malfunction, plan for it, and design around it. Without this thinking, bridges would collapse in high winds, buildings would easily topple in earthquake zones, and aircraft wings would fall off in the high stress of severe turbulence. However, we must guard against analysis paralysis or we will never move forward before yet another meeting is had, a form completed, or a bureaucracy satisfied. Airplanes wouldn't even exist if Black Hat thinking alone ruled the day.

De Bono also introduced the Yellow Hat, an optimistic mindset that considers that success is a serious possibility. This success orientation can fuel the spirit and energy of an entire team, especially if they know it is not reckless optimism but instead balanced by the other five hats.

As Menlo grew, we began to formalize more of our employment processes. You know the drill: an employment manual, tighter employment agreements, and so on. Mel, our attorney from the big law firm Dykema, provided wonderful support during this process. Lawyers, like engineers, are paid to use the Black Hat view with their clients to protect them against unforeseen calamity and risk.

Mel suggested including various clauses in the employee handbook and the agreements, and often James and I would say no, explaining the culture we built and why those standard approaches weren't going to be needed. Mel would pull us back and explain the risks involved. James and I pushed in the other direction and told Mel that those were not concerns for us. We recognized the risks, but we also recognized the risk of promoting a certain kind of culture to our future employees and then presenting documents and guidelines that looked exactly like those of all other employers.

One such clause was to protect us against employees making disparaging remarks about Menlo in any of a variety of channels. This is an incredibly important consideration, especially in the context of social media. We told Mel to drop the clause from our contracts. He balked. We pushed back, and eventually it was dropped. This kind of back and forth continued until one day we had a breakthrough moment with Mel. He looked at us across the table, and said, "Would you guys mind if I had my daughter apply for work here?" He finally saw the benefits of our optimism.

Were James and I being irrationally optimistic about the legal entanglements that can occur in an employee-employer relationship? Maybe, although, those who know James Goebel well would never accuse him of irrational optimism. Me? Guilty as hell. This is what makes us good partners. I am Tigger, he is Eeyore.*

What James and I both refused to do, though, was expend loads of energy planning for negative outcomes in regulations and rules. Our belief is that as soon as you post those notices, the team takes note and believes they are seeing what leaders really feel is going on. This may increase the work of leadership from time to time as then there is no easy rule to fall back on. Instead there is the hard work of talking, listening, and thinking. James and I also believe by treating our team members with dignity and respect we will avoid a lot of what the lawyers worry about.

The Crossroads of Leadership and "That's Not How We Do Things Here"

Where do joy and optimism intersect and how do we balance them against fear, the reality of running a business, and staying safe? Welcome to the hard work of leadership. You didn't pick up this book thinking it was going to be easy, did you?

Many executives and their team members come to visit Menlo from all over the world. They come in droves from the biggest brands in business: GE, GM, Ford, Mercedes-Benz, Toyota, Vistaprint, Steelcase, McKinsey, Coca-Cola, Liberty Mutual, Mass-Mutual, OppenheimerFunds, USAA, TD Ameritrade, Morningstar,

---

* Go watch James Goebel's compelling TedxTraverseCity talk to learn about joy from the Eeyore perspective. You will love it.

DENSO, Walmart, Discover Financial Services, Nationwide . . . the list goes on and on. They fly in, many on corporate jets, to spend a day with a small, humble team in the windowless basement of a parking structure. They leave having witnessed a different way of working, and, often, they are inspired. They want something we have. Inevitably, a visitor asks me what simple thing could they do as leaders that would make a difference in their organization?

"Move out of your office and turn it into a conference room" I tell them.

Nervous laughter usually follows. What about private conversations that we leaders need to have? they inquire.

"About what?" I ask.

More nervous laughter. As you might imagine, most don't take me up on this idea.

One did. Ron Sail, now retired, was the leader of GE Global Services in Schenectady, New York—a part of the company's shared services operations. Ron heard me speak, read *Joy, Inc.*, and came to visit our offices. When he got back to Schenectady, he was so inspired by our way of working that he promptly gave up his office, tore down walls where the rest of his team worked, and moved into the open with the rest of his team. He adopted other Menlo practices, including High-Speed Voice Technology (eschewing electronics and actually *talking* to one another), daily standups, and visual management, and in that transformation he reinvented an employee services unit of a large company. Now others at GE want what Ron created. The kind of leadership joy that Ron captured in his division is catchy.

Ron is one of those rare leaders every one of us would want to work for. He embodied the humility and gentleness any one of us would want in a "boss." I got to visit him in his reinvented environment at GE just a week before his retirement. They had just named a training center after him. I met the amazing team he led, and saw the love that team had for him. The fact that this occurred within the company founded by Thomas Edison was just that much more delicious for me. (In case you missed it, we named our company in honor of Edison's Menlo Park, New Jersey, invention factory.)

Ron chose optimism. He brought his entire team along on what could have been a scary journey because he believed good could come from it, and it did. He and his team stopped using "that's not how we do things here" as a crutch from transforming into a better, more trusting, more joyful workplace. So why can't you try it?

Get Moving

Begin your pursuit of joy with optimism. Try something new in your daily routine or way of working. It can be anything—the important thing is to "run the experiment" and believe that positive change can come from it. Keep moving forward.

I ran a 10K in the summer of 2017 at the encouragement of my second daughter, Lauren (we call her Lou). I was turning sixty that year. For the few years prior, I had run a mile at least once a week, more in the summer. I had also run a few 5Ks a year, and this would be my second 10K. Still, I wasn't ready for the race. I hadn't trained for this distance. I signed up anyway. I completed the first 5K in good time, made the turn back, and started walking. I was tired, a bit sore, a little bit out of breath, and my legs were heavy. Others around me were still running. Some were older than I; others appeared less conditioned. I picked it up again, and then walked again. I *think* I ran the last 5K more than I walked it, but it was close. As I reflected on my performance I came to a few conclusions:

I outran everyone who didn't come to the race that June Sunday morning.

With a little more practice, I could eliminate the walking.

I didn't need to walk; I wasn't about to collapse or anything.

I can do better. I will do better. (Thanks, Lou, for the inspiration and motivation!)

I was proud of my accomplishment, but more important, the experience gave me new goals: to run farther before walking. Make it the whole way. Do a half-marathon next. Dream about a marathon.

Stop contemplating and get moving with the optimism that you can accomplish something great. Heck, set this book down right now and try something new. If you need some optimistic inspiration, go find someone in your company or in the world and start running alongside them for a bit, figuratively or literally!

I believe that thousands of people come to visit us every year because they want to see what running toward joy looks like. How does optimism play out? Where did it hurt? Where do you slow down and catch your breath? Were you struggling as much as you anticipated, and was the decision to slow down driven by actual need or simply a lack of full belief in your ability to run the course of change?

Optimism Is Fueled by Courage

Just as joy and happiness are not the same, neither are optimism and enthusiasm. For one, optimism requires courage.

Choosing optimism is scary; you worry about coming up short and failing to meet expectations, either your own or that of others. If we hesitate, or equivocate, we also run the risk of failing to inspire others to be courageous and take risks. We end up in an environment where the Black Hats win the day and every conversation isn't about what is possible but rather about what is safe.

As Rollo May famously said, "The opposite of courage is not cowardice, but conformity." If you do everything the same as everyone else, you can't possibly be blamed if things go wrong. If you take a chance and step out on a limb, the limb could break, and others may see you fall. But if you do try, you outperform everyone who didn't take the chance you did. That puts you ahead of 99 percent of the population. This is what courage feels like, and how optimism is fueled.

I witnessed this kind of leadership courage at one of the nation's oldest companies, 165-year-old MassMutual in Springfield, Massachusetts. One of their key leaders, Dalton Li—a former navy nuclear submarine officer, McKinsey consultant, and then head of Lean Enterprise Practices at MassMutual—had read *Joy, Inc.* and came to visit us at Menlo several times. In late 2016, he invited me to keynote an internal MassMutual leadership conference they called Getting Better Together.

I spoke about all facets of Menlo culture, ending my talk with a story about how we welcomed babies into our offices, an experiment that had dramatically positive and unexpected results for the culture at our company.* "Run the experiment," I said, and then see what happens. "Don't wait for permission or bureaucratic buy-in. Don't ponder all the possibilities. Try it and see what happens."

This is how I have ended a hundred *Joy* talks around the world. The message seems to resonate, and teams have shared their own stories of putting this to work in their cultures. I've gotten a sense it has inspired those who heard it. However, I could not have predicted the impact these words would have on MassMutual.

In June 2017, six months later, I was invited back to meet with hundreds of leaders and staff around the company. Every corner I turned, there were copies of *Joy, Inc.* People greeted me as if we were old friends. All over the company, in two cities and two states, I encountered a notably different and energized MassMutual. I

---

* I tell this story in full in *Joy, Inc.* but some brief background: In 2007, Tracy, a Menlo employee, was getting ready to come back to work after maternity leave. There was only one small problem: what to do with three-month-old Maggie? The day care she planned to use was currently filled, and grandparents lived too far away to help for an extended period.

I told Tracy that she should bring Maggie in to work. She questioned my sanity, assuming it would never work. I told her we should run the experiment and, despite her misgivings, she brought the baby to work with her. Though we weren't necessarily set up to be particularly "baby friendly," it worked beautifully. Tracy prepared a small sleeping and feeding area for her and Maggie. If Maggie fussed, Tracy, or more often, another team member, picked the baby up and held her.

Tracy's courage to run this experiment, while continuing to be a contributing member of our team and juggle the challenges of being a parent of such a young one, is a testament to the type of leadership we encourage at Menlo. And as of this writing, we have had twenty-two Menlo babies in the last eleven years. Most have been brought to work for weeks or months, by moms *and* dads.

couldn't believe what I was witnessing. Was it really possible that a company as large and as old as MassMutual could make so many changes this quickly because of one simple exhortation?

Amy Ferrero, VP of Claims, took me to the claims department, kind of *the* big-deal department of an insurance company. The department is a massive operation, occupying tens of thousands of square feet—just what you'd imagine in an insurance company with nearly $30 billion in annual revenue. As we walked the floor, I noticed that dozens of helium-filled balloons, the kind you'd expect to see at a child's birthday party, dotted the landscape above the low office walls. Remember, this is a serious, legacy life insurance company.

"What are all these balloons doing here?" I asked.

Each balloon was attached to the desk of a staffer who was inspired to run an experiment, Amy told me. She encouraged me to walk over to any person whose desk had a balloon and ask about the experiment they ran. I spoke first to Erica, who told me her balloon came from a proposal to process simple life insurance claims faster than the typical four-week turnaround period. She and her colleagues tried out a new system to deal with claims that had clear identification and a single beneficiary—getting their transactions down exponentially. Their record so far? Thirteen minutes. Unbelievable.

I found great joy in witnessing the pride, ownership, accomplishment, and infectious enthusiasm in Erica and the team around her. I felt as if I were witnessing the birth of a joyful leader, who had the courage to run an important experiment, and one that, so far, was quite successful.

Later that day, Dalton showed me a simple diagram of their journey to lasting change. It has the elements you'd expect: develop awareness, build understanding and skill, bring it all together, share your mastery. Good stuff. But Dalton and his fellow leaders took an extra step I'd never seen before. They added *inspiration* at the very beginning. They decided that no change will begin unless it begins with inspiration. Brilliant. In this case, that inspiration fueled their energy to run the experiments I was now witnessing.

This might seem trite but consider how many corporate-change initiatives begin with an announcement, often via email, that the company is embarking on a lean transformation, an agile transformation, a pursuit of Six Sigma quality, or some other buzz-word of the day. The management edict notes that employees will be trained on new tools, books will be purchased and distributed, new software installed, and so on. You can almost hear the simul-taneous laments of the seasoned workers who've been through this before—*Here we go again.* What is left out is the deeper "why" be-hind any of these changes. How does this change connect to our purpose as an organization? A team needs inspiration to get to optimism. Once they get it, they will move mountains or hoist he-lium balloons in ardent commitment to a change they were led to believe in.

Joyful leaders are optimistic. They step into the danger. They take chances. They run experiments. They risk failure and set-backs. And in all of this, they inspire others. Anyone who aspires to leadership dreams of inciting such inspiration in others. And then they take the steps necessary to envision that inspirational journey for those they lead.

CHAPTER 5

Visionary

> Your vision will become clear only when you can look
> into your own heart. Who looks outside, dreams; who
> looks inside, awakes.
>
> **—Carl Jung**

It is February 11, 2027, at about eight o'clock in the evening, and Menlo's celebration of Edison's 180th birthday is well under way.

This is probably the most anticipated day in Menlo's history, as the planning for this day started way back in 2016. This is a pivotal day in our ten-year vision because we can now actually compare where we are to where we thought we would be ten years ago. It seemed impossible at the time that we could set a sight so clearly and come this close to achieving what we had set out to do. Of course, the vision itself inspired us along the way and informed us. That's what visions are supposed to do. We just had no idea that we could do it.

To keep the vision alive over the last ten years, we crafted many different versions and formats to make it meaningful and approachable to everyone on the team. We finished off the screenplay version, created a fun picture book, and created several video vignettes that have turned out to be very useful in our marketing efforts. The vision, once completed, drove our website redesign and actually led to the inspiration for a very different marketing effort and focus for the company. And though some of the specifics changed over time, it resembles the vision we dreamed of so many years ago.

Those gathered for our big party include current Menlonians, now numbering well over two hundred (more than we had envisioned), and their families as well. There are so many friends from times past, including community members who have cheered us on over the years, former Menlonians who wouldn't dream of missing this party, customers past and present, and two still-active founders, Rich and James. Also attending are well over three dozen entrepreneurs who can trace their beginning directly to the Menlo effect. Some were coached by Rich and/or James, some hired us as their design and development team, some camped in our Startup Garage and adopted their favorite aspects of our culture. What is most delightful for us, is that the sum total of their revenues and employees collectively exceeds Menlo's . . .

So began a draft version of Menlo's 2027 vision. (The final version of our 2027 vision can be found on the Menlo website.) The vision statement describes our growth path, the kinds of businesses we will be in, our customers, the effect we have on the world around us, the very personal impact we've had on current and former employees and their families. It also paints a picture of how we have helped our community and helped grow other companies. It describes our next office location by size and layout. The vision also describes the things that are still the same. For example, James and I are still involved and still sit out in the open space with the team. It outlines the experiments we've run and how that has changed the nature of our business over the years.

The ability to envision the future is as essential to leadership as the ability to articulate it in a way that is inspiring to others. A concise and compelling vision simplifies the decision-making process for specific endeavors and continually reminds us of what is important and what isn't.

A leader's vision must be both *very* personal and shared by others. On the surface it would seem as if these two are contradictory. Will all personal visions be inspiring enough to others for them to adopt them as their own? Of course not. Yet a leader's vision must be big and inclusive enough to motivate a team of people to help make it come true. A hollow, selfish, personal vision won't be very inspiring and might be followed with the motions of your team but not their emotions. In short, there must be joy for others in your vision. No joy, no followers.

Our company vision is tied to our mission, our purpose, our culture, and the systems and processes that bind them all together. Our mission has always been to "end human suffering in the world as it relates to technology." Our purpose and goal are to return very real human joy to technology. This drove us to create a culture with a joyful external focus: to delight the people we serve with compassionately designed user experiences and solidly engineered software. We knew this also required a joyful internal focus, to bring together a high-energy team whose very essence is worthy of learning from and seeing firsthand.

All of this would be supported by a process that never felt heavy or bureaucratic. Our envisioned processes would lift the burden of the work rather than add to it. It would simplify decision making; give concise clarity about effort, organization, and progress. The regular and frequent visibility into actual progress would inform tradeoffs and direction. We chose to share everything we learned with willing students from around the world, so that those so inclined could make significant change in their own teams, working shoulder to shoulder with them to help them achieve their own version of joy. All of this is hard work, but it would be so satisfying given the effect the work would have on people everywhere.

It is not enough to simply *say* you want to have a great culture. It requires so much more than motivated personal intention. Most failed culture initiatives look exactly like late January at the local fitness club, suddenly and remarkably empty after a brief and intense launch.

Intention requires action, structure, and persistence. It requires clarifying your vision of a better future. It requires understanding the basic human behaviors that make things work and prevent change.

A strong vision can imagine a great culture, but culture without process leads to chaos and process without culture yields soul-crushing bureaucracy. Culture structured around a process, where everything is focused on producing your version of joy, engenders two kinds of joy: in the world of those you serve, and in the team itself.

Most organizations are supremely organized around day-to-day operations. Phones ring, you answer. A sales lead arrives, you follow up and create a proposal. A problem arises, maybe even something as straightforward as a plumbing issue, and someone calls maintenance and it gets fixed. The lights go on in the morning, the coffee is brewed, the dishwashers are emptied, the day proceeds, and at the end of the day the dishwashers are loaded and started, and the lights are turned off and the doors are locked. At night, the cleaning crew empties the trash and cleans the floors. Each day's pattern follows the next.

Amid this practical and useful busyness, how do we move forward? How do we reimagine and reinvent ourselves? This is where a well-communicated vision plays a key role.

The visioning process itself should be inclusive, not the exclusive domain of the owners, founders, or C-level brass executives. In creating our 2027 vision, we regularly invited team members to visit with James and me during the writing process. We had them edit portions and add their own views on the future. I used these sessions to ask team members to tell me in their own words what they appreciate about Menlo, why they want to be here, and what they hope for in the future. These freewheeling discussions were inspirational for me and fueled my writing as I listened.

Establishing a vision doesn't have to be a hurried process. After all, why hurry when the day we are imagining is ten years from now? However, we do need to proceed with diligence and effort in crafting our vision, applying energy to it just like in our normal day-to-day. There should be a beginning, middle, and an obvious end to the visioning process itself.

Then what? How does the vision itself stay alive for the next ten years? So much of this kind of planning work can easily be tucked away on a hard drive, distributed as an email attachment, read once, and then archived. There can be a C-level presentation to the team, but these one-and-done events have a limited shelf life. And what of the staff members who join the day after the vision is presented? How are they brought into the process?

If it is stored away in a document-management system and never retrieved, it cannot stay alive and change the course of history for your company. To correct this, we have built elements of our vision into our weekly FOOBB (Financial Operations Open Book Board) meetings, so that the entire team is reminded weekly of the metrics we are pursuing and how those metrics connect to the activities of the business. If someone new wonders "Hey, where did these numbers come from?," a team member can point them to the vision.

All this falls under the domain of leadership. The visioning process must be kept alive—and this is one of the key responsibilities of leaders. The specific results and achievements will be different than originally imagined, but we must be able to identify and acknowledge the elements of the vision coming to life as we move forward.

Now, setting a vision is still a new and active process for us. (Ask me in 2027 how it all went.) But we are very fortunate to have a local compelling example of the power of visioning with Zingerman's. We enthusiastically followed the Zingerman's model for visioning, which encourages two things: hot penning (just start writing and don't stop until done) and picking a specific moment in the future and describing it in drippy detail. Iterate until complete.

Cofounders Ari Weinzweig and Paul Saginaw wrote the first formal vision for Zingerman's in 1994, when the company consisted of just one deli and one bakehouse, with combined annual revenues of $3 million and a few dozen employees. In their vision, Ari and Paul took an ambitious look fifteen years into the future, writing that "Zingerman's would be a community of businesses"—all unique enterprises under one brand based in Ann Arbor.

By 2009, fifteen years after this original vision, the company had grown to include Zingerman's Roadhouse, a creamery, a mail order business, a catering division, coffee and candy companies, and a training company. The organization was bringing in $50 million in annual revenues, employed more than five hundred people, and had been feted on the cover of *Inc.* magazine as "The Coolest Small Company in America." Pretty great for a small local company, right?

While I can't tell you exactly whether our vision will come to fruition as well as Zingerman's did, I am already seeing practical and tangible ways our team is bringing the vision into the day-to-day operations. After we shared our initial vision, Lisa and Carol asked James and me about our 2027 revenue target. Their basic question was, "How are we going to make that happen?" I'm pretty sure James and I waved our hands in the air at first and expressed some bland platitudes about systematic growth and diligence, blah, blah, blah.

Lisa and Carol, being the task-oriented professionals that they are, felt that our seventy-thousand-foot view of this wasn't going to actually happen unless it was present in the day-to-day. Lisa drew up a year-by-year revenue chart that showed straight-line revenue growth from today to 2027, so we would know what 2017 needed to look like to get to our ten-year target. Then the team produced a bar chart, separated into revenue categories, that is updated each week at our Open Book Finance meeting. Carol took it a step further and embedded the week-to-week revenue numbers into our financial projections on our Open Book board.

Now we were faced with the excitement and stress of seeing how we are doing on our ten-year plan week by week. For Carol and Lisa, these were fundamental acts of leadership based on a vision, and this vision was used at first to hold James and me accountable. When 2017 ended up with the company meeting about 70 percent of goal, we were asked how 2018 would be different or if we were satisfied with this result. (Dang, there is that inconvenience of accountability!)

In response to these questions from the team, we started the Liberty project to *systematically* track every sales activity we have going on. We established a sales management process that relies on both a paper-based visual management system and an electronic customer-relationship-management system. We also began to hold a biweekly review (akin to a Show and Tell) to examine every lead and the associated follow-up actions. Now our vision is manifested in the day-to-day in the sales arena. I see similar initiatives happening in other circles when it comes to expense management, strategic investments in marketing, staffing plans, and proactive sales efforts. In short, the vision is embedding itself in the way we lead.

Vision at Every Level

The focus of this chapter to this point has largely been about a company-wide vision established by and protected by founders and a CEO. However, the visioning process does not need to be restricted to the CEO's office. If someone has an idea for a change at Menlo, we ask, "What is your vision for that change?" These visions don't have to be as elaborate as our ten-year vision and can have much shorter time horizons. It would make sense if they somehow relate to the bigger vision, but even that isn't an absolute requirement. (If they contradict the ten-year vision, that will likely not work without much greater buy-in, of course.)

In early 2017, Lisa H., one of our longtime team members and project managers, drafted a vision for the *Menlo Bits*, our monthly newsletter. This exercise took her around an hour and a half. Since we are now past the due date for the vision coming to pass, I added in what actually happened. You'll note we pretty much fell short of every target and that's OK. The vision inspired us to make positive changes, and every metric was improved significantly.

MENLO BITS 2018 VISION

It's January 2nd, 2018 8:00 am and the first Menlo Bits of the new year has just reached the inboxes of subscribers in the EST time-zone. By the end of the day, it will have reached the inbox of just over 4,000 people! That's 1,000 more than this time the previous year, quite a significant jump, when you consider that in the past, our subscriber-ship has increased by about 500 people per year. We did our part by offering the chance to receive our newsletter to Menlo visitors, class attendees, and putting it on Rich and James' slides at speaking engagements. But we were surprised to see that much of the growth came from our current readers recommending the newsletters to colleagues, friends, and family because they found it so valuable, providing insight and ideas on a regular basis that inspire, encourage, and inform.

We plan to see this number rise even more as Rich has included an invitation to join the Menlo Bits to readers at the end of his new book (look for this near the end of the book!). One of our goals for 2018 is to focus on how to further increase international member-ship of the newsletter, as the majority of subscribers are from the United States.

Over the past year, we have gotten to know quite a few of these readers by name, through their feedback, conversations in regards to articles and stories we have shared, and through other experiments we have run as we seek to develop the Menlo Bits not into just a newsletter, but a cohesive community of people located across the globe who share a passion for joy in work and life and who we help connect together to explore meaningful topics, pursue passions, and learn from each other.

We have even started to keep track of what we know about our readers so we can find ways to stay connected with them in the future and sometimes even delight them in a way they wouldn't expect. As a result of what we learned during the 2016 Advent calendar experiment, we were able to wish Jahn of Cologne, Germany happy birthday on December 17th and we sent Pagan's 12 year old son (an avid fan of Joy Inc.) a copy of Rich's new book.

The Menlo Bits has also become a place where we can generate leads for potential work and classes through the relationships we have with the readers. We were also able to trace the Advent calendar event to $9,000 of sales for Menlo as a number of class spots were purchased from some of the individuals we offered gifts to. Something that was harder to measure, but another outcome of the experiment has been further relationship building with some of the companies we have been connected with over the years, some of which has even led to some booked business. At least 3 presales conversations, an Influencer class, and an HTA project were in some part a result of the Menlo Bits.

We have also followed up with our readers, over the months, some who received free visioning content, some who learned how to create their own persona map, some of whom we gave a copy of a book we recommended. These follow-up conversations sometimes led to further learning and relationship building and in one case, a private tour.

We have gotten more intelligent about what kind of content our readers are drawn to and have been doing a better job at maintaining interest in the newsletter, which has helped to increase the percent of people who actually read the newsletter each month. We have also continued to include more and more original content in each newsletter. Sometimes this has even included storytelling from members of our team about challenges, learning, and new experiments at Menlo. We have also found ways to make the text we share with the readers "punchy," to be playful, yet serious about what we are seeking to get across.

We have also noticed that more and more of the new clients we have at Menlo stay connected with us during the engagement through the Menlo Bits. We have noticed that some of the subscribers with the most opens and clicks are from companies that are current clients. There have even been a few cases where an existing client will ask a question about something they came across in the Menlo Bits to our team after a Show and Tell and the team gets to have a great dialogue with the client.

We have tracked the following for this year of the Menlo Bits:

- # of Subscribers: 4,100
- % of subscribers who open the newsletter each month: 40%
- # of subscribers we have engaged with during the year: 225
- # of experiments run in the newsletter during the year: 10
- Dollar amount brought in by the Menlo Bits (via classes, Amazon book affiliates program, booked business, etc.): $25,000

Being that the Menlo Bits now brings in some revenue, we have established a small budget for the Menlo Bits in 2018, to be used for giveaways and other promotions to engage our readers, and run some other experiments. We look forward to seeing what the next year of the Menlo Bits brings and how it enhances both the Experience and Client Work aspect of the business.

Here is what actually happened:

- # of subscribers: 3,417
- % of subscribers who open the newsletter each month: ~30%
- # of subscribers we have engaged with during the year: ~25
- # of experiments run in the newsletter: 7
- Summer Reading Program
- Theme-inspired newsletter
- Changing the editor of the newsletter each month
- Sharing Menlo Vision with them
- Allowing them to ask questions of Jeff Kupperman
- Run a survey to learn about classes
- Offer them a chance to win a free spot in class if they forward *Bits* to someone else
- Dollar amount brought in by the *Menlo Bits* (via classes, Amazon book affiliates program, booked business, etc.): ~$9,000

No one asked Lisa to write a vision for the newsletter but she felt compelled to do so because it was important to her, and because she knew it would be embraced by our culture and our team. And while she felt personally invested in its fruition, she didn't make it only about her. You can see that there is no "I" language in the vision. This is a selfless vision and that selflessness invites followership. She doesn't now need to go tell people to help her carry out the vision. The vision will carry itself. In this way, visioning helps ease the process burden of leadership.

My friend Stan Slap wrote a wonderful book about leadership in the middle-management layer of big corporations called *Bury*

My Heart at Conference Room B. What Stan discovered is that most middle managers don't have a chance to live out their personal values at work, so they end up being one person at home and another person at work. Home usually gets the better, more authentic version. Work gets the outside of the mask. If we can tap into the heart of individuals, however, we can get to the best they have to offer.

Lisa looked outside to dream about how to make the *Menlo Bits* a better version of itself for the readers. She also looked inside the company and made sure there was enough there to make the changes sustainable for the company to continue to invest in this effort. Finally, Lisa searched her own heart and imagined what would bring her joy in this vision for the *Menlo Bits*. She wanted to be in a better relationship with readers, to make the newsletter audience more personal with Menlo and with each other. She wanted to improve the team's relationship with the readers and connect the joy of readership with the joy of being Menlo.

Now, while vision is important, it is also important to tie all this back to realistic expectations. It's necessary to stretch ourselves, but if doing so causes us to overreach, then a vision doesn't get anywhere past the paper it is written on.

CHAPTER 6

Grounded in Reality

I always like to look on the optimistic side of life, but I am
realistic enough to know that life is a complex matter.

—Walt Disney

I LOVE MORNINGS, ESPECIALLY IN ANN ARBOR. THIS IS A TOWN
that loves to sleep in. If you get up early enough, you pretty much
own the town. My alarm goes off at 5:35 a.m., and I'm usually to
work by 6:30 a.m., and an hour later on Mondays, Wednesdays, and
Fridays when I work out. I am almost always the first or among the
first to arrive at the office in the morning.*

---

* Yes, joyful leaders may need to put in a bit of extra time. As CEO, COO, and founders,
James and I do try to keep our work to nearly forty hours, even for our leaders, but
often miss that mark. That said, I am happy to report I protect evenings and weekends

I start my mornings by flipping the On switch at Menlo. There are quite a few light switches to hit, and I have a pattern that brings sunrise to our basement space, no matter what time it is. If there are cups or dishes lying around the space, I'll grab as many as I can while making my rounds. After I hit the kitchen lights, I check if the dishwashers have run, and if so, I empty them. If there are dirty dishes in the sink that didn't make last night's run, I refill the dishwashers and clean the sink. If I decide to stay in the office and not hit one of the local coffee shops, I'll fire up the first pot of coffee and maybe put on some music to fill the space with my favorite tunes. I then sit down, with my steaming cup of coffee, freshly brewed, and start checking email.

It would be easy to hire some support staff to take care of these details or simply pass it off to other team members. But, I enjoy the practical reality of attending to this level of detail at our company. It reminds me that while there is visioning, speaking to others about our company, and flights to faraway places to meet new and interesting people, there are also the very, very practical tasks that make a business run and a team move forward. Some of those tasks aren't glamorous, they aren't lofty, but they are necessary. I think it's important, as CEO and leader, to stay grounded to these necessary realities of business.

---

for family. James seldom misses his kids' soccer and volleyball games, unless he is traveling. We leave early together on summer Tuesdays for our golf league.

Cultural Custodian

Ryan Sullivan is the founder of A2 Functional Fitness. When founding his most recent venture, he spent a lot of time focused on creating an intentional culture. Much like me, he had witnessed firsthand how toxic broken cultures can be, and he didn't want that for his new company, an amazing boutique fitness center near the Ann Arbor Airport. (Full disclosure: I am an investor in A2 Functional Fitness, I train with Ryan, and he is my son-in-law.)

In his business plan, he called out the role of *Cultural Custodian*. I love that title. He lands the responsibility for this role squarely on the shoulders of the founder, CEO, or top leader.

Here is how he describes it:

The Cultural Custodian: This is the person that manages the space, schedule, cleaning, maintenance, day-to-day business, and culture of the organization. Any issues with anything involving the core Cooperative will be addressed by the cultural custodian. In a traditional business model, this person would be a director or CEO. Good leaders are servants of their communities. For this reason, the cultural custodian is charged with providing balanced value to each and every member of the Collective. This Pillar acts as the guardian of the organization rather than a director, and is why part of the job duties of the cultural custodian includes cleaning and maintenance of the facility. It is his/her job to care for every aspect of the Cooperative.

Do you see how grounded Ryan's thinking is here? In addition to the duties of founder and visionary leader, he is taking on the very real and humble goal of custodian, since those details matter to him and to his vision to the point that he doesn't want to simply delegate them.

If you want to set a tone for your organization but only speak to it every once in a while in a rah-rah speech and don't live the exacting life necessary to be intentional about your culture, the kind of culture you seek will fail to take hold and that failure will drive the rest of the team's attitudes and behaviors.

Reality Matters

In an earlier chapter, we explored the courage of choosing optimism in the face of fear. I fully believe in that, but I also recognize that optimism alone is not enough. The practical realities of business cannot be avoided. Run out of cash and you die. Stop listening to your customers and your market withers. Stop watching the numbers and recovery may not be possible. Fail to establish simple, repeatable systems and the organization will devolve into chaos.

As of 2017, Menlo is still a small business of fewer than fifty team members. Some ask us why that is—why aren't we bigger after sixteen years? I'd love to have a glib answer to that question as if it doesn't matter to me, but it does. I suppose in my head, we should be bigger: more people, larger office, more revenue, and higher profits.

As I mentioned earlier, while 2015 was a year of amazing growth, 2016 was not. The year 2017 started and stayed strong until the end of the year when slowness hit again. We cannot deny this reality. We can't make it go away. What we can do is look at the reality straight on and do something about it. Leaders do not wither when times get tough.

In 2016 we got very serious about Open Book Management, letting everyone in the company peer into the numbers—every single one of them. It wasn't pretty. Cash was dropping, and the first seven months of the year were not profitable, though, thankfully, the last five mostly were. We decided to keep the team in place for better days to come. This was trading one form of business pain for another.

Reflecting on this time, there could not have been a better time to get very serious about open financials. We needed everyone's help. It scared some team members a lot, though fear was not the goal. We had to figure out how to ground our next steps in reality.

Using an example from college football, when my beloved Michigan Wolverines lost a tough game to their in-state rivals from East Lansing, football coach Jim Harbaugh had this to say:

"We're going to put steel in our spine. They [the players] played really well, competed like maniacs, both teams did. It was a heckuva game. Played winning football. Didn't get the result. Welcome to football. Move forward."*

---

* Angelique S. Chengelis, "Harbaugh Says UM Will Put 'Steel' in Its Spine after Numbing Loss," *The Detroit News*, October 17, 2015. https://www.detroitnews.com/story/sports /2015/10/17/harbaugh-says-um-put-steel-its-spine-after-numbing-loss/74160570/.

We needed to remind our team not to be fixated on our past results. "Welcome to business. Move forward," essentially became our mantra. As we honed this message and our results improved, we started to build more resilience among our team as well.

We found joy in surviving tough times. We saw the abyss of business, survived, and now thrive again.

We will see a dip again. One is always down the line. We won't like it. It won't feel any more comfortable. But we will be slightly less scared of what comes next. We will know that we are at our best when we come together as a team and face the reality together.

Joy, Optimism, Reality, Fear—The Leadership Stew

High on the walls at Menlo are posters of our own creation. These display our most precious maxims. One of our most popular is a Frank Zappa quote: "The computer can't tell you the emotional story. It can give you the exact mathematical design, but what's missing is the eyebrows."

Alongside this one is one of my most popular quotes: "Fear does not make bad news go way. Fear makes bad news go into hiding." Some people interpret this as "anything that produces fear is bad." I couldn't disagree more. While, as a leader, I would prefer not to motivate with fear, it can in fact be the best motivator under the right circumstances and conditions and within the right culture. What we should not do as leaders is try to motivate by producing *artificial* fear.

Real fear—the kind that keeps us from walking out into the

street without looking both ways first, that tells us to buckle up, not text while driving, wear a life preserver while boating, and know where the closest exit on the airplane is—is the fear that actually keeps us safe and alive. These are healthy fears. I want the team to be afraid of running out of cash and not making payroll. I want them to fear injuring a patient if we make a mistake when creating software for a medical device. Within this fear is great responsibility: to be good stewards of everything given to us, whether our work, our customers, our revenue, our profits, our reputation, our team, our equipment, our building.

One of my earliest lessons of understanding and harnessing fear came as a sixteen-year-old on a fun boat outing with my high school best friend, Doug. We had spent the day boating on Lake Huron, the second largest of the Great Lakes. As the day was winding down, it was time to take the boat back to port, a few miles up the coast. Quite suddenly, the weather changed; the rarer east winds that can whip the lake into a frenzy were kicking up fast. The small craft was bobbing up and down with each swell. We needed to slow our pace to keep everything under control. I was swallowing hard at this point, as I'm sure Doug was. We began peering along the shoreline to see if there were any other viable landing alternatives. There weren't. We would need to make it all the way back to the safety of Port Lexington.

There was another problem, in addition to the weather: our full day of playing had consumed a lot of gas, and the rougher, slower pace wasn't making this situation any better. Doug couldn't see the gas gauge, since it was behind him. I was the only one who could see it. He asked me how we were doing on gas. As the boat pitched and bobbed up and down the swells of the ever angrier Lake Huron, all I could see was the needle smacking against "E" again and again. He needed an answer. I contemplated what I should tell him and the effect my answer would have on his piloting.

"We are just fine. Plenty to make the return," I told him with confidence.

I had no idea if that was true. I didn't *know* the truth. What I did know is that I didn't need to increase his fear about getting us back to port. He had plenty already. I also knew we had no other choice but to stay the course—and that Doug was a capable and experienced boat captain. In the end, it all worked out, though I'm pretty sure we made it back to port on fumes alone. When we docked, Doug checked the tank and, seeing it was empty, asked me why I didn't tell him. "What good would it have done to know?" I replied. He smiled and thanked me.

My inner engineer wants an algorithm to determine the right balance of optimism, realism, fear, and hope to motivate my team. I want a crisp, clean answer as to when to do what. When to inspire, when to command, when to let others make mistakes without oversight, when to share the reality for exactly what it is at the moment. I also want to know when to shade the reality with optimism, born out of the wisdom of experience, to say everything is going to be OK even if I don't know exactly how.

As leaders, we need to balance the reality of current business results with the optimism that no business ever grew without taking some chances and not every risk taken succeeds. When times get tough, we need to inject optimism based on stories we've collected over the years when we survived earlier scares.

This is perhaps one of the hardest leadership truths: you need to be exactly the leader the team needs you to be when they need you, really need you, and you won't be. Not all the time. It's not humanly possible. When you're not, apologize. Part of the balancing act is allowing your own humanity to show. You may want to be a superhero, and sometimes you will be, but there is Superman-crippling kryptonite everywhere. Sometimes Lois Lane and Jimmy Olson—the regular, bumbling friends who loved, admired, and supported Superman—will be the regular folks who surround you and rescue you with their compassion and caring. Let them. It's OK. Superman needed a team too.

When Caution and Growth Meet in a Dark Alley

In our earliest days, we occupied a fun little storefront at 212 North 4th Avenue in downtown Ann Arbor, right on the edge of the Kerrytown area that includes some of Ann Arbor's most delightful and eclectic shopping and eating treasures.

The office itself was wide open, with high ceilings and bulletin-board material on walls, where we posted our paper-based visual management system of pushpins, index cards, colorful sticky dots, and yarn. It is still amazing to me how much work we got done in that 2,000 square foot storefront. Even then annual tour counts often exceeded 1,000 per year.

My old boss Bob Nero (former CEO of Interface Systems, where my joyful pursuits began) had become the CEO of a firm that provided insurance regulation compliance software to some of the largest insurance providers in the nation. In his new role, he was a potential client and I was excited to work with him again, doubly so because Bob directly knew the value of our approach based on our work together at Interface Systems. It felt like a slam-dunk that we'd win their business. Upon visiting our office space, Bob asked a question that clanged loudly in my brain: "Rich, how will you fit our project in your tiny little storefront?"

Bob could see that the space was already filled with the people needed for our current book of business. He knew the project he was contemplating for us would need more people, and he could do the visual math and see that a bigger team wouldn't fit in the space, that we wouldn't be able to scale to meet his needs.

We didn't get the business in the end, but we got something far more important—an honest and unvarnished evaluation of our baby. She was cute but needed to grow to be competitive in the next rung of business.

I went to our CFO and cofounder Bob Simms and told him we needed to find a bigger space if we wanted to grow the business. We scoped out a space nearby that would triple our footprint and our rent. We were month-to-month in our current lease, which gave us tremendous flexibility and entailed very little risk. The new space would be a six-year lease—a big commitment for a fledgling firm.

I said, "We have to do this." Bob said, "Not possible." I said, "We need to grow the business." He said, "Grow the business and we'll be able to afford it. We were at an impasse.

Bob and I were at odds. Yet, both of us cared deeply about the company and wanted success. What was there to argue about?

Why couldn't he see my point of view? It comes down to the fact that we are wired differently and that the values we instinctively retreat to are in direct competition with one another, especially in times of conflict.

The Competing Values Framework, developed by the Center for Positive Organizations, is a useful model to lean on in these situations. This model teaches us about four quadrants of values:

Green: the Imagine Quadrant, which sees value in new ideas and innovations, regardless of cost; innovate or die.

Red: the Control Quadrant, which sees value in process, procedure, and quality. For example, expenses should be watched carefully, or we could run out of cash.

Yellow: the Collaborate Quadrant, which sees value in teamwork and relationship, that the team at its collaborative best can meet any challenge.

Blue: the Compete Quadrant, which sees value in speed and authority, because those in authority can make speedy decisions. They don't mind stepping on toes to get things done, because winning is more important than good feelings.

Bob wanted the certainty of knowing we could afford the new space. His simple idea was "Rich, go win the business, and then let's talk." (Red.) My view was, "We'll never win this new business or anything else substantial until we get the new space. Besides, it will be so exciting!" (Green.)

Our third partner, James, was more in the middle on this one. He could see the opportunities and the problems. He believed that we could work this out as a team. (Yellow.)

In the Competing Values Framework, Green (Imagine) is juxtaposed with Red (Control). Taken to extremes, these two categories of people really don't like each other. They don't get along. They wish the other didn't exist. That wasn't the case with Bob and me. We both appreciated the value the other brought to the table. It was a civil and reasoned disagreement. We both believed the other when we argued that the disagreement was existential for the company. We wanted what the other wanted.

Enter Ann Arbor SPARK, the local economic development agency of our fine city. I approached them about a loan, a rather modest one of $25,000, that we would draw down as we needed it, but never more than $2,000 per month—just enough to cover the initial difference in lease expense. Bob negotiated a lease with our new landlord that tipped up over time—less expensive in the beginning years, and more expensive as time went on. *Voila!* We signed the lease and tripled our space. We drew down about $18,000 of the loan and then paid it all back in one payment in less than a year after moving in. Six years later we tripled our space again, without needing to take out a loan.

As this example shows, where there is productive tension between healthy competing values, there is progress. If one of these values wins out and drowns the others out, there is trouble. We need healthy conflict between these values to grow, much like we need exercise to get stronger. Together we will make better, more innovative decisions.

Note that though our situation was a showdown between Red and Green, the strongest leadership teams include people who are associated with the Yellow quadrant (Collaborate) and Blue quadrant (Compete) as well. Without diversity of beliefs, we will struggle to confront the realities of running a business. If we don't confront the realities, winning will be academic and the subject of countless articles about a failed organization and "what could have been."

Turn Outward

The realism required to run a joyful business for the long term requires healthy amounts of all the values mentioned above. The natural conflict between values also must occur in healthy ways. If the conflict becomes aggressive, or passive-aggressive, or is simply ignored, we will flounder and bad politics will become the norm. Most wish to escape such an environment.

This balance is hard, and we won't want to work this hard without a greater purpose in mind. To win in the long run, we must ultimately turn our attention away from our business and ourselves and look outward. The outward mind-set appeals to the deepest aspiration and wiring of human communities: *service to others.*

CHAPTER 7

Servant Leaders

I slept and dreamt that life was
joy. I awoke and saw that life was
service. I acted and behold, service was joy.

—Rabindranath Tagore

IN THE SUMMER OF 1968, MY MOM ORDERED A HUGE NEW BOOK-
shelf for the living room. She was very excited, as new furniture
was rare in our house. Though we were comfortable, money for
nonessentials was tight. This bookshelf came in a box and required
assembly.

One evening, as the unopened box sat out in the garage, Mom
and Dad went out to dinner and a movie (which was unusual for
them). I wanted to surprise them, so I went out in the garage and

pulled out the thirty wood pieces and the nearly one hundred nuts, bolts, and screws. Dutifully following the multipage instruction manual, I put that bookshelf together, all by my ten-year-old self.

Then it dawned on me, I had built it in the garage and Mom wanted it in the living room. Undaunted, I decided to move this massive bookshelf, right where I knew she wanted it. I inched that thing out of the front of the garage, turned the corner with it, inched it downed the sidewalk, into the family room, through the utility room and the kitchen and into the living room right where she wanted it. I quickly set up Mom's knickknacks, some of Dad's books, wired up the stereo, and I had one of Mom's favorite records playing when they walked in the door. My dad was speechless. Mom cried. *Joy.*

For many years, I thought joy in business, as I found it, was related to my earliest experience with technology. From Singapore to Berlin to Paris, when people asked me where my joy came from, I would tell them about discovering programming in 1971 and the joy of typing a two-line program into a computer and it clacking out "HI, RICH" on a teletype. But the more I thought about it, I realized that interaction was only a small part of my joy. I remembered that bookshelf story and it occurred to me . . . joy comes from serving others with the work of our hearts, our hands, and our minds. That's the true source of business joy.

I've always wanted to delight other people with the abilities I was given. This is, in fact, the heart of the engineer. We love to build things not for ourselves but for others. The real joy I pursue in business is the same joy I felt when my mom cried on seeing the bookshelf I built for her.

Often our biggest challenge in leading is how we define success: for ourselves, for others, for our teams, and for our companies. If we get the definition of success right, leading becomes much easier. You can unleash joy within yourself and the team. If we pick the wrong definition, we have a harder job than Sisyphus. We are pushing heavier and heavier rocks uphill every day, and if we stop pushing, those same rocks roll right back over us, and we are crushed.

If you consider some of the best business stories you've ever heard of you will likely see a pattern emerge. A team will work so hard, so diligently, and perform above their paygrade when focused on something worthy, something bigger than themselves, and something that isn't about self-gratification but about serving others. As leaders we must first see for ourselves, and then envision for others, what kind of joy we wish to deliver to the world.

When I am asked by our myriad visitors where to start such a leadership journey, I suggest they begin by defining the kind of joy their team wishes to deliver to the world. This journey begins by considering one critically important question: "Whom do you serve?"

This seems like such a simple question. It isn't. The three obvious answers—our customers, our employees, and our investors—actually miss the entire point. A heart of service directed at those obvious stakeholders is still "self-serving." Of course, we serve our customers; they are the ones who provide our revenue and ultimately our profit. Of course, we serve our employees; they do the work necessary to serve our customers well. Of course, we serve our investors; they provide the capital necessary for serving the other two groups. We do want to serve all these groups.

In order to identify to an inspiring and lasting version of joy, we must look further than those stakeholders. If we don't, we run the risk of chasing only profits, awards, and recognition, or big stock-price gains.

You've probably heard the oft-told story of the three bricklayers. They were working, all three laying bricks, when a curious passerby asked what they were doing.

> The first man answered gruffly, "I'm laying bricks."
>
> The second man replied somewhat proudly, "I'm putting up a wall."
>
> But the third man said enthusiastically, "I'm building a cathedral."

I'd like to take this just a bit further. It is likely in cathedral-building days that the third bricklayer would die before the cathedral was complete. He would never see the results of his labor. But one day that cathedral might be the spiritual home of his children and grandchildren. His endeavor was worthy because he knew who he was serving and that his work was bigger than him.

Consider a life insurance company. Whom do they serve? The easy answer would be they serve policyholders. And yes, that is true. But there is little joy derived, beyond commissions, by selling the next policy. Selling policies is the lifeblood of the organization.

A life insurance company serves people they will seldom ever meet and people who will never pay them a single dime: the *beneficiary* of the policy. In fact, at the moment of first contact, their customer has passed on, and the person on the phone is looking for tremendous service and potentially a big check. The person on the other end of the phone line is most likely in a moment of great need. They have just lost someone who is very dear to them. They may have been financially dependent on that loved one, and their life partner was thoughtful enough to have purchased a policy to protect someone they had formerly dedicated this life to. This stranger is now calling the life insurance company expecting compassion, understanding, thoroughness, organization, and care. They have a story to share, a sad one, and they have hope that the person answering the phone fully understands how difficult a time this is. Delivering that service well can produce joy for your team beyond measure.

Imagine how different this would be if such a company decided to outsource claims handling to the cheapest provider possible and instructed them to assume fraud as a first line of defense in every conversation. This is what happens when we substitute service for efficiency.

As we think about joy at Menlo, our instinct is to delight the end users of the software we create. They don't know who we are, and we will likely never meet them. They don't pay us for what we do. We typically build software for a company that wants to sell their product into a market. Yet one day, if everything goes well, someone will tap on a screen or click a button with their mouse and thus touch the work of our hearts, our hands, and our minds. We want them to delight in the experience.

We also think hard about all the people we work side by side with as our clients. We recently finished a contract project with a client who has worked shoulder-to-shoulder with us for a couple of years. The team will do the remaining work themselves. One of the owners of the company sent the following note once the cap-off was completed:

> Although I am so proud of our IT Department and their confidence and ability in our team to finish the rewrite of our legacy software, we cannot discount the value Menlo has been in getting us to this point. The professionalism Menlo has brought to us has been top drawer in every aspect of our relationship. We will always be grateful and most appreciative of Menlo support.
>
> Judi

Joy.

It is an interesting exercise to think about "whom do we serve" for any business. Start with yours.

Is Your Company Too ＿＿＿ for Servant Leadership?

Many who encounter us are envious of what we have accomplished but know it is out of reach for them because they are too ＿＿＿. (Fill in the blank . . . big, small, young, old, regulated, and so on). It is almost as if they are saying, "We will get to servant leadership once we ＿＿＿ (achieve profitability, leave this place and start our own business, retire and work for a nonprofit, or on the weekends in our volunteer efforts)." Or they think that their business isn't a place for servant leadership because all effort at work needs to be focused on winning.

I don't believe this, and neither should you. There is always room for service to others and the leaders can set the tone to drive this point home.

One of my dietary weaknesses is a McDonald's Quarter Pounder with cheese, accompanied by a large order of fries and a Coke. I eat this only when I travel, and mostly at airports. (Please don't tell Jes, my fitness trainer, about this!) I'll sometimes grab this combo at my home airport.

At the McDonald's in the Delta terminal of Detroit Metro Airport, there is an older man, Mike, who cleans up after the busy travelers, emptying the trash, wiping the tables, and sweeping the floor. I've seen him again and again, and his attention to detail and diligence is always the same. That to me is remarkable enough, but Mike does something else even more remarkable; if he notices you don't have a napkin, he'll ask if he can get you one. Then he'll chat you up about something and finish by wishing you a great and safe flight. I often found myself thinking, *What a remarkable person, to bring this kind of effort and attitude every day to work. They are so lucky to have him (and so am I!).*

One day, I went there for my favorite combo and Mike wasn't working that shift. Another, much younger man was performing Mike's job and was wheeling out a big load of full garbage bags from the back. He went right by my table. Then an astounding thing happened . . . he asked me how I was doing and whether I needed a napkin or anything else. He then wished me a safe flight before continuing his journey to the dumpster.

I have eaten at many (too many) McDonalds and other fast-food restaurants in my life—and this behavior stands apart from all others I have ever witnessed. The first time Mike did it for me, I thought maybe I just caught him on a good day. But he did it every time I was there. OK, so Mike's just a nice guy. I get it. Then the young worker did the exact same thing. Is it possible that the two nicest guys (one younger, one older) in the fast food industry just happen to work in one of the least relational places (a busy international airport) on the planet? I'm having trouble believing it is a coincidence.

Mike no longer works there, but I tracked down the manager of that McDonald's on one of my subsequent trips (and favorite meals) at Detroit Metropolitan Airport. I asked about Mike and his kindness. He thanked me for noticing. He told me they were in a highly competitive environment and a little kindness and caring can go a long way to getting people to change their choice.

Do you still think you can't make any changes at your company or in your department or in yourself? Think again.

If you could bring joy to a franchise of one of the largest fast food empires in human history, particularly at a place as transient as an airport, full of busy people impatiently rushing from city to city, you can do it in your team and your business. That servant leadership attitude can start anywhere and with anyone.

Teaching Servant Leadership

Leadership author Lorin Woolfe says it so well:

> The ultimate test for a leader is not whether he or she makes smart decisions and takes decisive action, but whether he or she teaches others to be leaders and builds an organization that can sustain its success even when he or she is not around. True leaders put ego aside and strive to create successors who go beyond them.

Once we have a clearer picture of who we serve, and what delight looks like for them, we leaders must make that joyful intent clear to those on our team. This can't be done in a one-time speech or a poster on the wall in the lunchroom. It must be lived and breathed every day. We will serve our teams by defining joyful service to others in our specific context, but to truly serve them, we need to teach them how to look for this joy in their own day-to-day work.

A few years ago, we opened our doors to a local church that wanted to use our space in the evenings to teach a course on financial freedom based on the materials of Dave Ramsey and his Financial Peace University. The course was open to the public, and two of our team members, Anna and Kealy, took the class with others.

Anna's and Kealy's lives were changed by the course, and they decided they wanted to bring that change to others, both on our team and in the community. They signed up to become instructors and offered the class again in our space in the evenings. They plan to repeat this program in the future.

Kealy and Anna decided to take time out of their lives to serve others, some of whom they knew, and others they didn't. They have helped many others make their financial lives better as a result. This is exactly the kind of servant leadership that we need to see more of in our work. Whether inside of work, through outside volunteerism, or both, we must continually encourage and support our budding leaders to practice servant leadership. The more we can get them to feel the power of serving others, the more they will want to practice it everywhere in their lives.

There are so many different opportunities for servant leadership inside of an organization. It would be fun to consider establishing a norm of "How can I serve others today?" Some ways can be small and quick, others requiring more thought and effort. The example of Mike and his McDonald's coworker could have been coincidental; it may have been limited to these two staff members, and when they left, their servant leadership example went with them. And that would have been sad. The challenge with all the good things we do as leaders is, how do we build the practices in our daily work so that they sustain over the long term? How can we ensure that servant leadership doesn't just rest with a single leader, but is imbued throughout the organization and becomes the great responsibility and privilege of people across the company?

To answer that question, we need to explore what it means to create a culture of leadership.

PART II

Building a Culture of Joyful Leadership

CHAPTER 8

Start with Purpose

My story is a freedom song of struggle. It is about finding one's purpose, how to overcome fear and to stand up for causes bigger than one's self.

—Coretta Scott King

The Wisdom of an Eight-Year-Old

In the 1990s, there was a popular movement afoot to take your children to work with you for a day. I recall this started out as "Take your daughter to work" day. Whether sons or daughters, the idea was the same: show young children what Mom or Dad does at work in the hopes that it might inspire them to career dreams of their own, motivate them to stay in school, and lead them to healthy, happy, productive lives. At worst, your precocious kid could get a day off from school and spend some time with Mom or Dad somewhere other than home.

In 1997, just after I was promoted to VP of R&D at Interface Systems, I took my then eight-year-old daughter, Sarah, to work with me. She came fully prepared for an exciting day at work with her dad with a backpack full of crayons, markers, stickers, and coloring books. Seemed appropriate to me. After all, what is there to actually see when watching a VP work?

She sat at the task table in my big office, happily coloring away and meeting many of my colleagues when they came into my office to meet with me. She sat there all day while I answered phone calls, checked emails, wrote status reports, and laid out the next week's plan for my team.

At the end of the day I told her it was time to go home. We both gathered our day's work, mine into my briefcase, hers into her backpack. Almost out of obligation to her school and teacher, I asked her, "How was your day, honey? Did you learn something today about Dad's job?"

"Yeah, Dad," she replied. "You are really important."

Oh my.

I grabbed the chair across from her, slowly set my briefcase down, and took a seat. Of all the answers I could have expected, this was the least likely in my mind. What could she have *possibly* seen that would lead her to this conclusion? This warranted a deeper dive.

"Why would you say that, Sarah?" I asked. "What did you see?"

"Well, what I saw is that no one here can make a decision without asking you first."

She was very proud of her dad.

I was mortified.

In this moment, I realized that I had created a team and a system that couldn't move faster than I could, the boss. If I worked harder, stayed later, took fewer vacations, stayed electronically tethered to the office, my team could move faster. This was a lose-lose-lose scenario.

I lost because my only option was *work more hours*. This was not my desired outcome. In fact, this was the very reason I originally resisted the promotion when it was first offered. I did not want to sign up for the time obligations required for a VP of a public company. My family was way too important to me.

My team lost because I was slowing their personal and career growth. I was continuously at the center of every important decision. This was limiting their opportunity to improve decision-making skills and negatively impacting their leadership development.

My company lost because they weren't getting the best every team member had to offer. And those team members, who were still getting raises every year, didn't have the best chance to add more value as time went on.

I continued to reflect on the wisdom of my eight-year-old in the days and week ahead. I saw a pattern in my history. I had always liked being seen as the smartest guy in the room. I likely drowned out the answers of my peers at critical moments in group settings. This led to promotions and raises; my efforts were rewarded, sometimes handsomely. I was following the example of those who preceded me. Everywhere I worked up to this point had demonstrated the same behavior: elevate the heroes. If I wanted to gain ground, move up the ladder, I needed to be and act like them. What other examples did I have? None. It was the same everywhere.

But what was my actual reward? Time away from family. Sleepless nights. Less than stellar results based on the dollars expended. Yet, there continued to be accolades and further rewards, including more stock options.

My solution to this tension was always to work harder. Double down on the hero thing. What other route was there, after all?

Plan B

Now, there were alternate narratives I was just beginning to understand. Several major threads connected at the same time to show me what a different route of leadership—not just being a boss—could look like.

The first: My wife, Carol, had started working for a management consultant, Kathy MacDonald of The MacDonald Group. Kathy had a wonderful library of business books, and each time I visited Carol at work, I would ask Kathy for a recommendation. Wisely, Kathy asked what I was struggling with, and she would put the appropriate book in my hand. This led to great impromptu discussions about culture, leadership, and modern management techniques. Our conversations spurred me to revisit books from my past that had initially inspired me, books like Tom Peter's *In Search of Excellence*, which gave me a peek into very different high-performing innovation teams like those at 3M. I reread Peter Senge's *The Fifth Discipline—The Art of Practice of the Learning Organiza-*

tion, which had instilled in me a desire to pursue better systems, better forms of communication, and faster feedback loops. I was also reminded of the very first business book I had ever read, Peter Drucker's *Management—Tasks, Responsibilities, Practices,* which drilled home the point that among the most important things management really needs is a flexible workforce, not a single person who saves the day for the company.

The second: Around this time, a video cassette showed up on my desk from one of my programmers, Bob Johnson. It had a handwritten label: "The Deep Dive."

I took it home and watched with great fascination as the team from the news program *Nightline* visited IDEO, an industrial design firm in Palo Alto, and filmed the team there trying to reinvent the tired old grocery shopping cart in just five days.

In that now-famous episode, Ted Koppel, the show's host, introduced IDEO with an opening that really spoke to the heart of what I wanted to pursue: "It used to be you deferred to the boss. It used to be you were supposed to climb the corporate ladder. Well, forget the way it used to be . . ."

As the segment proceeded, I saw a totally unique example of the kind of change I was seeking personally, professionally, and corporately. At IDEO, there were no titles or permanent assignments. Seniority didn't determine who led project teams. Instead, leaders were chosen based on merit and skill. Hierarchy was seen as harmful to the innovation culture. People who merely listened to the boss weren't helpful; IDEO wanted people who disagreed with the boss. Everyone sat in an open office space together, the opposite of my team's quiet corridors of cubes and offices. The whole team brainstormed together; there was no waiting for one boss to come up with the next great idea. Much of what IDEO did was anathema to corporate America at the time—and I was intrigued.

I was so excited after watching the video. It felt like everything was falling into place and I could now clearly see my plan B escape route. I began to consider the possibility that I could work and lead in new ways. For the first time in a long time, I began to see a way out of my boss-led, meeting-heavy, lengthy-process, slow-decision, high-chaos environment. When I went to the office the day after watching the IDEO video, I asked the executive team if I could have thirty minutes to share this video with them at the next meeting. This was a bold move on my part, as I was still the new kid on the block with the executive team. The kid wanted thirty whole minutes of the executive team's time to watch a video? Seriously?

Fortunately, the executive team gave me the time, and when the day came, I wheeled the TV and VCR into the boardroom, turned off the lights, and played the episode for the other executives. If I could have, I think I would have held my breath the entire time. I couldn't imagine what would have happened in my head had they scoffed. But they didn't. They got excited too. Even my harshest critic, Keith, the VP of Sales, who counted on my team to make good products to sell in the marketplace (which we didn't), asked me, "How soon do we tear down the walls?"

The third: Within a couple of weeks of my airing the IDEO video with the executive team, one of my fellow VPs, Brian N., dropped off some brochures about an Ann Arbor–based company called AppNet. AppNet offered a program called T.E.A.M.—

Training, Education, and Mentoring—which was described as a facilitated consulting engagement that would bring my team into the modern technical age of object-oriented programming, which was all the rage at the time.

A few days later I was in an AppNet seminar, learning for the first time about an emerging practice touted by Kent Beck, a West Coast programmer turned writer, dubbed *Extreme Programming*. These practices were an outgrowth of an iterative and incremental approach to software design and development that would eventually be codified in the *Agile Manifesto*.

His practice was so different from the approach I knew—interactions over processes, collaboration over negotiation, and so on. Perhaps the most intriguing aspect of Kent Beck's approach was that it advocated for a collaborative approach to software development called pair programming. Two developers worked on the same machine, shared a keyboard and mouse, and developed code *together*. I was deeply intrigued.

I now had strong inspiration and even stronger motivation to make a big change at work—to change not only how I approached work but also how my entire team thought about their jobs and their roles.

Within a few weeks, my team joined me in trying a new way of working that eventually evolved into a new culture and a very new approach to leadership in the organization. To begin, team members moved out of their offices and cubes into an empty part of our moth-balled printer factory, a space we dubbed "The Java Factory," because we were going to be experimenting with building Java-language–based software. To get team members to trade working the old way, in isolation in their cubes, for the new method, paired programming in an open office, I told them that the only way they could work on new products would be to do so in the new space and in a new style. The siren call of new product development was too exciting to turn down.

We also brought in some new friends from AppNet to help us work through this new, paired programming system. This is where I met my eventual Menlo cofounder James Goebel; he was the lead consultant from AppNet.

Soon, team members started experimenting with new ways of working and interacting. There weren't a lot of rules, and the level playing field of everyone having the same "office" seemed to foster a spirit of camaraderie, equality, and trust. We were all learning a new language together and a new work style together.

Crucially, because it was all new to me as well, I didn't have any special "power" as the boss anymore. Traditional management was fading, and leadership emerging in its place.

I knew it was working when I realized that the team was starting to solve problems without me.

About six months after we started working in the Java Factory, I was walking the halls at Interface Systems when one of my programmers, Dave L., called out to me.

"Hey, Rich, we had an emergency today," he said. "But everything's okay, it's all taken care of. I'd be happy to tell you about it if you want an update."

Wait, what? Emergency? What emergency? How could I not have known about this? Why wasn't I being apprised of the event, brought in to help, and kept up-to-date on minute-by-minute progress? Why wasn't I being called on to make a decision, solve a crisis . . . be the boss?

As I was learning to let go and become far less of a manager and far more of a leader, my team picked up the pieces that in the past would have come crashing down to the floor. Now I could marvel at how fast my team was moving, with me or without me. My daughter Sarah might have been disappointed with my new lack of importance (although I doubt it), but I couldn't have been more thrilled.

It worked phenomenally well not only for me but for the company overall. Interface Systems became a darling, named the No. 1 public company in Michigan by the *Detroit Free Press* thanks to our meteoric stock rise. A highflying Redwood City, California, firm, who loved how my team worked and wanted it for themselves, acquired the company. There were plans to grow the Ann Arbor operation to over three hundred people, and I would be leading it all. Hooray! It was a wild ride and it was about to get even wilder.

You know this story now: the bubble burst, the NASDAQ came crashing down through five thousand, and my dream was dashed. By April 2001, it was all done as they and most other Silicon Valley firms had lost 99 percent of their overinflated value. I lost my job and was applying for unemployment.

Yes, it was all gone, save one thing: what I had learned in those two years about leadership, process, teamwork, and what could result from such a collaborative environment. I learned that by reminding a team of a meaningful purpose, and intentionally building culture and systems around this purpose, we could move faster and my work as a top executive could change dramatically and joyfully.

I was determined to do it again, as were the people who became my cofounders in Menlo Innovations—James Goebel, Tom Meloche, and Bob Simms (all from AppNet). We haven't looked back since. Tom left after a couple of years to pursue his own big ideas, and Bob retired in 2016, so James and I now hold the candle for the dream we worked so hard to create in 1999 at Interface Systems.

An Intentional Culture Is Both Established and Emergent

In this part 2, we'll dive deep into how we built a culture of leadership—an environment and ecosystem where many people, not just the CEO, feel accountable for the organization's performance and help direct it to new heights.

I want to note that in our world, a culture of leadership manifests in a nonhierarchical office. We did not set out to build a bossless workplace, although that is what we became. We never read about Holacracy, or Teal, or any of the other popular terms used for flat organizations.

We also did not set out to become a Lean company. The Lean community discovered us and told us we embodied lean thinking. Same with Deming, Six Sigma, Agile, Scrum, Design Thinking, Influencer, Getting Things Done, Outward Mindset, Toyota Kata, and so on.

When I say this, people look at me and remark, "But Rich, you said you created an *intentional culture* and yet it sounds like you just stumbled into most of what you have now."

Both things are true. The intention and purpose of our culture was as clear at the beginning as it is now—to "end human suffering as it relates to technology" by bringing joy back to the invention of software. We had a purpose from the start—and that purpose dictated everything that we built.

Everything we chose to do, from paper-based planning to weekly cycles, to pair programming, to open office plan, to daily standups, to teaching our Menlo Way to others, to tours, to writing books, to Open Book Management, to visioning, and yes, to avoiding a dog-eat-dog, get-to-the-top-of-the-heap-and-defend-your-position management system, were all sought in the pursuit of an intentional culture.

Most of the things we do now that we are admired for evolved from some very simple experiments. Those that succeeded became more intricate over time. We will change and be different years from now for the same reason.

I will say this clearly and briefly: *Do not pursue process, plans, or practices without purpose.*

You can't embark on a journey to establish a culture of leadership for its own sake. Your organization must serve a higher purpose. We figured out that at Menlo we wanted to produce joy in the world for others. The things we do are in pursuit of that joy. Bringing joy to others gives us pride in what we do. That brings *us* joy.

A purpose-driven culture is hard to build. It takes time. You will suffer setbacks, you will be mocked until everyone says what you do is just obvious, and some people will expect immediate results while you are rebuilding the airplane you're flying in. Remember that you're doing it for the right reasons. And it will result in joy.

Most of us are willing to work very hard for something important. Ask anyone who has stood alongside a loved one through a
chronic illness. Some ask, "How did you do it?" You might answer,
"I don't know *how* I did it, but I do know *why*."

You Can't Do It Alone

I am not a strong enough leader, even with the weight of my CEO
title behind me, to do this alone. This is where purpose steps in to
carry the day and the team.

If I can light the flame of strong and worthy purpose in the
hearts of those around me, they will begin to carry that flame even
when I am not around. Critically, they can light the flame in others;
they can begin to lead without me. That's how a culture of leadership emerges.

This initial flame can be sparked from anywhere in the organization. It does not have to begin with the top guy or gal. It can start
with you, wherever you are. My flame-lighting journey to joy
started long before I was a VP and even longer before I was CEO.
There's no reason to believe that other, very capable leaders live in
your organization, waiting to emerge. They might just need you to
bring them out by providing them with an appropriate purpose. Do
this and regardless of what your organization does, in what industry, and with what workforce, you can evoke capable leaders.

More Important Than Ever

The first world has shifted from a muscle-based economy to a brain-based economy. The disparity between these two economic worlds is painful to watch. Even now, the brain-based economy is under assault with the advent of rapidly expanding machine learning and artificial intelligence.

I believe we are now witnessing a shift from a brain-based to mind-set–based economy. As author Carol Dweck explains in her book *Mindset*, individuals possess either Growth Mindset or the Fixed Mindset. The Growth Mindset helps us process and succeed in a rapidly-changing world because we assume if we don't know how to do something, we can learn. The Fixed Mindset, on the other hand, can set us back on our heels, rendering us unable to keep up with the rate of disruptions because we have an inflexible idea of what we are capable of.

While Dweck focuses on the individual, I don't think it's a stretch to say we may be witnessing the same divide applied to teams and organizations. Organizations that learn to adapt and change rapidly will be the most likely to thrive. Organizations that use the old hierarchical, do-only-what's-best-for-shareholders-above-all-else model will fail rapidly. We see evidence of this in the daily business reporting about the old, lumbering organizations that are shrinking, closing, and dying.

A growth–mind-set economy demands speed and distributed, near-the-work decision making. It demands adaptation. A flatter structure satisfies the need for increased speed by removing delays and lifting very smart workers out of the bureaucratic despair of endless meetings. This does not mean all standards are thrown out the window: a bright frontline staff still needs overall values-based guidance (aligned with a purpose and driven by vision), fenceposts (guiding principles), a broad behavioral compass (expectations for critical behaviors), instructive lessons (that inform and teach visible actions), and an easy-to-navigate process (systems thinking) so that *small mistakes* can be *encouraged*, caught early, and corrected while there is still time and money to recover.

This last point about "making mistakes faster" is perhaps the most important for the adaptation required for a growth mind-set-driven organization. Organizations must have systems for trying new, uncomfortable things, failing quickly, learning, and growing.

We also need to avoid artificially manufactured fear techniques like table thumping, raising voices or eyebrows, or rolling eyes. In short, trust needs to be built through relationships. In all of this, leadership can, will, and must emerge—in every corner of the organization.

This growth will feel as painful as a newly implemented personal fitness routine. You'll be slow, winded, and sore, and you'll frequently wonder why you are doing all this work. Legendary San Francisco 49ers football wide receiver Jerry Rice said it best about his own grueling workouts:

"Today I will do what others won't, so tomorrow I can accomplish what others can't."

Leadership is the glue that brings it all together. The challenge you'll have is that you won't find a pool of talented leaders whom you can just plug into your culture of purpose and run with. You will need to create an environment and system for finding talented individuals, building them into leaders, and giving them space to flourish.

CHAPTER 9

Value Leaders, Not Bosses

If your actions inspire others to dream more, learn more, do more and become more, you are a leader.

—John Quincy Adams

WHEN THE NASDAQ BEGAN ITS AWFUL SLIDE IN DECEMBER 2000, the CTO of the company that had acquired Interface Systems warned me that cuts were coming and that I should be thinking about whom to let go when asked.

Somehow I got it in my head he was talking about four or five people. A week later, when he called again, he told me to cut *half* my team.

"By when?" I asked, after a long pause (once I started breathing again).

"I need the decision by noon," he said.

It was 10:00 a.m.

He needed the names to pass on to HR that afternoon, so they could prepare exit packages for half my team, to be delivered right after Christmas break. The CTO didn't offer any help in making these wrenching decisions to lay off people I liked and trusted; he had other calls to make.

It was one of the loneliest moments of my professional life. I closed the door to my office, took a deep breath, and started making a list. One by one, I went through every member of my team, considering each person and their performance. Each one of these souls was vital to the success of the Java Factory, and part of an amazing family. The boss part of me had a tough decision to make. The leader part of me couldn't help but consider the weight of the decision I was about to make and how those decisions would play out in the home lives of each of the employees. I also knew they would all wonder *Why me?* and *Why wasn't I one of the half who got to stay?*

A couple of weeks later, the HR team arrived from headquarters and split my team into two groups. One went into the cafeteria to learn their fate, receive their exit packages, and be given a few moments to ask questions. The other group was led into another part of the building to hear the fate of their peers and give those now-former peers some privacy as they packed up their personal items.

I went into the room with the team members who were being let go. It was difficult to watch as they learned of the decision.

Like a sturdy sailing ship, my career had carried me well to this point. Sometimes I was steering, sometimes I was riding along and enjoying the view. Yet, in this lonely and stormy time, I was the captain, confronting the stark contrast between a boss who had to make a tough decision and a leader who had to care for his crew. I was personally going to be OK (for now), yet I now had two groups to care for as best as I could: the first—those losing their jobs—and the second—the shell-shocked remaining half of the team who were losing so many colleagues in an instant. I would soon learn the strength and resilience of the team we had built and the resilience of a culture of leadership.

One of the team members being fired, David E., took out a yellow note pad and scribbled down some column headings on it. In front of the California HR people and me, he told the group, "Okay guys, sign your name here and put down your home email address. I will make an email group and we will support each other in finding our next jobs. If anyone hears who is hiring, send a message to everyone else."

My heart beat so proudly for this team. Even in a moment of despair, they came together so beautifully for one another. They showcased the strength of leadership and care for one another even in a somber moment.

That email group stayed active for almost a decade after that fateful day in January 2000. I know, because I was added to the group four months later when I lost my job, along with the other half of my team.

I grew up a lot that day. My boss side shrunk; my leader side grew.

Bosses Command, Leaders Influence

Bosses have a trump card that leaders do not have. Bosses can do the thing that our parents did that drove us crazy as kids. They can respond to "Why?" with "Because I said so!"

People who influence positive and beneficial outcomes, without the hammer of "Because I said so!" at their disposal, are good leaders, whether they are bosses or not. Bosses who use a "Because I said so!" approach are not leaders. Bosses can have short, quick solutions to complex situations. Leaders are not afforded that luxury. A leader must leave openings for conversations.

A leader when asked "Why?" understands that the question deserves a thoughtful conversation. A team member asking why may be afraid, may be curious, or may want to contribute ideas. Or they might not even ask a direct question but instead just make a quizzical face or look crestfallen when an idea is shot down. A leader's heart and mind must be open to all these possibilities and recognize that the person asking a question is a competent and caring team member and a peer, not a subordinate to be "managed."

A leader also considers that these questions represent opportunities to grow new leaders. Imagine, just for a moment, that the person asking why has spent a lot of time on their own *thinking* about the situation at hand. Perhaps they have an inspiring thought, but they don't know exactly how to express it because this leadership ground is new territory. They might have to muster the courage to bring their idea forward. They artfully waited for what they think is the right opening to raise a point, but they do it without finesse, as they are unpracticed in making persuasive arguments. This is a moment of great vulnerability. A leader empathizes and invites the conversation, both for the value of the conversation itself and the opportunity for growing a new leader.

If even a few of these interactions go wrong, a leader will assume the role of boss whether or not they want it. The spirit of a team member can be lost forever in these moments. Ironically, each time you lose a team member in this way, the boss's workload increases because one more set of able hands (along with a heart and a mind) is no longer available to help when really needed.

Does this mean those with authority should never make decisions without the consensus of those around them? Of course not. It is a lonely territory for leaders who are bosses (by decision or appointment) when sometimes there is no one else to turn to but yourself and God, and you need to make the best decision possible. These are often some of the most painful decisions you must make.

An Amazon search for "leadership books" yields over one hundred thousand results. That is Amazon's way of saying there are a boatload of books on this subject. The number drops in half if you search for "boss books."

I suppose each of these books offers a definition for what it means to be a leader, and many will likely differentiate between bosses and leaders. I am also going to guess if we added up all the definitions you'd find about bosses and leaders in these books, you'd quickly conclude that being a boss is "bad" and being a leader is "good." I disagree. There are good bosses, OK bosses, and bad bosses. Same for leaders. There are great bosses who are leaders, and there are great leaders who are bosses.

Let's dive into what it means to be a "boss." I think the key differentiator for the boss title is that it comes with some level of great responsibility. There may be legal or fiduciary responsibility, like that of being the CEO of a public corporation, or it may be that you are signing up for the visible results of an institution, whether you're the head coach of a football team or the president of a university. In these situations, if something goes wrong on your watch, you're to blame. If something goes really well, you *might* get credit. The blame-credit equation is nowhere near fifty-fifty.

This level of responsibility is the burden of being boss. As a former VP of a public company, and now as CEO of Menlo, I fully understand and empathize with the burdens of being a boss. Payroll, cash flow, liability, contractual obligations, and employment law are very real for my cofounder and me.

Bosses are also on the hook to get things done: launch a product, grow a company, increase stock price to satisfy shareholders, win a championship. Most of those activities require other people to execute the work. Bosses have two choices at this point: "tell" or "influence." If they simply use their positional authority and power to get things done, they are a boss, plain and simple.

This can work and can sometimes work very well. These bosses can be kind, they can be compassionate, they can be understanding. But when bosses "tell," employees are expected to listen and do what they're told. The less thinking the rank and file does, the better, in this situation. (There are certain circumstances when this approach is a really good idea; for example, if there is a fire, and the boss yells "Get out!")

If these same bosses use their influence to get others excited about the goal, give their team the latitude to decide for themselves how to get to that goal, support them in whatever way they can, and then get out of the way, they are using influence to lead a team of people to get those same activities done. In this case, bosses showcase trust, a belief in the competence of the people who work for them, and an inherent desire to see people around them take responsibility for what needs to get done. In such cases, the boss is also a leader.

In these same situations, there may be an individual (or a set of individuals) on the team who has no positional authority whatsoever but sees an opportunity to influence those around them to get to the goal. If they do this well enough, people follow their lead because there is trust and belief that this person is worthy of following. If there is no explicit authority when this happens, this person is a *leader*. This kind of leadership doesn't require title, authority, seniority, or tenure. It typically requires knowing people, both in a general sense and in a very specific sense; that is, knowing individuals and having a relationship with them. Trust is a necessary component of leadership.

Good Bosses, Bad Bosses

I've had good bosses and bad bosses. I bet you have too.

Bob Nero, who was CEO of Interface Systems at the beginning of our joyful transformation, tops my list on the great side. He set high expectations, held his entire executive team accountable in ways that rewarded good behavior, and discouraged the poor performance of just going through the motions and trying to get by. He was a great communicator with the entire company, the board, and shareholders. Bob also cared about his team members, got to know our families, had fun, got excited about golf and golf outings, and was also easily accessible.

Bob had a good bullshit meter too. In executive team meetings, he would do what I learned to call "core sampling," which is what drillers do to see if there is oil in the ground. If you told Bob there was oil in the ground—for example, that the company was going to sell $1 million in new product this quarter—Bob would drill a "core sample," asking, "To whom are we going to sell one million dollars of this new product, and what evidence do we have they are going to buy?" If you had a sensible, confident answer, he would move on. But woe be unto you if you didn't, because then the Nero core-sampling machine would start drilling holes all over your oil field.

I believe good bosses are worth their weight in gold. If you are a boss, there is nothing inherently wrong with being a boss. Your style, both personally and professionally, can make a huge difference to the performance of any organization.

In my very first job out of college, I had an experience with a very different kind of boss. I was asked to head up the effort to build an exciting new product. This is every software engineer's dream: to create something entirely new from scratch. Because of my youthful entry in the software world (I wrote my first code at age thirteen), I had already been programming for more than a decade by the time this assignment came along. My technical skills were top-of-game and I had already led smaller teams.

I was excited for this plum new team leader assignment. I met with my boss to discuss my plans and told him I'd like to go out and visit potential customers.

"Why?" he asked.

"I want to make sure we are building a product they will actually need. I want to make sure I'm solving problems they have," I replied with enthusiasm. Every engineer yearns for the opportunity to build a wildly successful product that people enjoy using.

The conversation escalated to argument, with the boss telling me that my "talking to customers" idea would not be necessary because marketing had all the answers I needed, and that our local subject matter expert was just down the hall to fill in any gaps. I made the mistake of pressing the argument. Exasperated, he scolded me and said if I were more interested in talking with customers than writing code, he would stick me in customer service.

My eyes lit up. "That would be a great idea," I said, "because I could actually build relationships with customers, really get to know them, hear about the problems they were having with our existing products and opportunities for improvement." I thought the experience could expand my horizons for what was possible for my new effort.

"You're not getting this, are you?" my boss replied harshly, looming over me. "If I stick you in customer service, you'll never come out."

I turned in my resignation two weeks later.

I had this conversation in 1984. I remember it like it was yesterday.

That boss killed a budding leader for his company that day. But he couldn't kill the leader *in* me. While that company didn't die immediately, it slowly declined over time. I can't help but think their trajectory had something to do with how they thought about bosses versus leaders. It was a shame, because for a long time it had been a *great* company.

Good Leaders, Bad Leaders

Leaders, like bosses, can be good and bad.

Bad leaders are self-serving, pretend to be the boss when they are not, express frustration without coaching, and react poorly to any bump in the road. They are very good at exporting drama to others. If there isn't enough drama at any given moment, they will invent some. They'd rather talk *about* someone than talk *to* someone. You hear them say "I" a lot if business is going well. But if things are going wrong around them, or they are not meeting expectations, it is always someone else's fault, and they spend time wondering when the ambiguous *they* are going to fix it.

Organizations with these kinds of leaders become highly polit-icized and distrust is common. At worst, people start hating each other. Good people retreat from taking risks, and if there are team members who are attracted to this kind of leader, cabals and cliques form. (There is often an oddly attractive charisma to this kind of leader, as naysayers are often perceived as more intelligent.)

Good leaders, on the other hand, are selfless, though they aren't martyrs. They pitch in where needed. They are humble and don't see any work as beneath them. They are not afraid of hard work. The work can be mental, emotional, or physical. They are as apt to clean up after a meeting as they are to facilitate and energize a dis-cussion during the meeting.

Good leaders are comfortable letting others around them lead. They don't shy away from conflict, but they don't fan the flames either. They know that life is ambiguous, and this doesn't throw them. If they see drama, they step into the danger of it and figure out what is really going on. They learn to trust the subtle cues that conflict is coming, and they respond accordingly to head it off. Yet they don't spend a lot of time worrying about what might happen, as they know they can rely a lot on the creativity and imagination of the people around them if it does happen. When problems arise, there is a spirit of problem-solving rather than an attitude of "I wonder who is going to solve THAT problem?"

Good leaders inspire others; they see the positive in situations and in people. They enjoy working through difficult problems and don't need to be seen as the hero. They derive inner satisfaction from the business going well. They don't treat praise like an accounting ledger that must always be in perfect balance. Things go better when they are around and it's not always exactly obvious why that is. If a leader is gone for a while, people are happy to see them when they return. They attract followers who want to be like them.

Good leaders are not all cut from the same bolt of cloth. Some can be cheery and optimistic all the time, others sanguine as needed. Some are serious and quiet yet instill confidence. Introverts and extroverts are equally likely to be leaders, and you benefit from both. Critically, leaders seek to understand people, are not paralyzed by people issues, and are able to maintain a healthy balance of the interpersonal versus tasks and work.

Now here's the rub: what I've described about good leaders and bad leaders is on a continuum. Every leader will fall somewhere on this spectrum from bad to good each day and over the course of a developing career. This is great news, because this means people are capable of change and moving toward the positive should they so choose. And good leaders will nurture the growth of other good leaders. The right organizational environment will foster the growth of a culture of leaders.

My experience tells me that bureaucracies and heavy hierarchies make this more difficult (though not impossible). Bureaucracy and hierarchy are to leadership development as drag is to an aircraft: the plane can still get off the ground, still get where it is going, but it will require more fuel and take longer. If we can lighten this drag on our organizational aircraft, we can fly higher, faster, farther, cheaper, and with less wear and tear on the plane, the crew, and the passengers. The people on the plane will arrive refreshed and more energized to take on the world upon the arrival at their destination.

Leaders, Leaders Everywhere

Bosses in an organization are easy to identify. Their title, their office, their box and lines on the org chart, and their *L* level in the personnel system allows you to count exactly how many there are. If you want to move up in such a hierarchy, you either wait until your boss moves up (or out) and maybe you get a shot, or you hope more boxes and lines are added to accommodate yet another boss.

I know someone who works at a big bank. He talks about meetings with his one-up boss, his two-up boss, and, on special occasions, with his three-up boss. He also knows *exactly* how many of these ups there are between him and the CEO.

The beauty of establishing a culture of leadership is that you can have as many leaders as your organization can support and sustain. You won't need HR approval, you won't need to buy new office furniture, build new offices, or invent new titles like Senior Executive Vice President.

First at the Java Factory and then at Menlo, we focused on building an organization that could move at the speed of the leaders, not the bosses. There were lots of leaders, in many different forms. Some quiet, some humorous, some serious, and some adventurous but all of them bringing expertise, excitement, and energy to the workplace.

Imagine what you might be missing out on by focusing more on bosses than leaders.

Bosses Don't Like Experiments; Leaders Do

You have likely heard the expression "It's easier to ask for forgiveness than ask for permission." I wonder if that is true in many companies. A boss-fearing culture will be a permission-seeking culture. And if permission is denied often enough, permission is no longer sought and new ideas will die before they are shared or acted upon.

In a strong leadership culture, in contrast, there often isn't a need for forgiveness and certainly not for the kind of permission we so often see in a boss culture. Mistakes happen quickly and are corrected early. No "blame committee" is formed. The organization as a whole can acknowledge a mistake, maybe even laugh about it, correct it, and move on to make their next set of mistakes—discovering, along the way, the kind of deliberate improvements and happy accidents that help move a business forward.

It took me awhile to get to a mind-set where I was perfectly OK with the poster we hung in the Java Factory at Interface Systems that said "Make Mistakes Faster." (We still have this original poster at Menlo.)

Were more mistakes really what I wanted or desired? No. I wanted fewer mistakes and more progress. I wanted more done in less time with the same number of people. I wanted faster, better, and cheaper.

It finally dawned on me that the ardent attempt to avoid little mistakes actually slowed operations down and led to the insidious big, protracted, costly mistakes.

A culture of leaders expects mistakes. In this environment, leaders are equipped to deal with problems as they arise, with little fanfare. They bring together teams to roll up their sleeves and work as a group to solve problems. They run new experiments to improve on old mistakes. At a certain point, you might begin to wonder if bosses are ever needed.

Leadership beyond Hierarchy

As I've shared, part of our business is teaching other people about the Menlo approach. We give tours and run seminars for thousands of people every year.

In 2008, we were asked to teach our approach to members of the IT team at Nationwide Financial in Columbus, Ohio. At one of our seminars, Cam W., an up-and-coming leader at Nationwide, asked a question we had never been asked before.

"Who do people report to at Menlo?" he asked.

I'd been teaching some version of this seminar for seven years and this question had never come up. I wasn't quite sure how to answer it as we had no org chart and no formalized hierarchy. I told Cam to wait for a minute and I ran out of the classroom, quickly gathered five of our team members and lined them up at the front of the class. I then asked Cam to repeat his question.

"Okay, who do people report to here?" he asked once again.

Oh, if I had only had a camera to capture the looks of the five Menlonians at the front of the room. They thought hard, looking up at the ceiling with their heads tilted and fingers on their chins.

"Well, I guess the process," said one.

"In some cases, the project manager," said another.

"Well, I guess, the customers, and the users we are helping them support," speculated another.

And then, almost without hesitation and in unison, they crossed their arms with fingers pointed left and right to one another, to say "We report to each other."

At this point Cam was convinced they just didn't understand the question, so he broke it down for them.

"Let's say you want to hire someone, who makes that decision?"

"We do," they replied, and briefly explained that in our Extreme Interviewing process, all hiring decisions are made by the team.

"Yeah, but who does your performance reviews?"

"We do," they replied, and explained our Feedback Lunch process.

"Okay, okay, but who makes the firing decisions?"

"Well, we do with loads of interactions with Rich and James. And if Rich and James feel the need to fire someone, they check in with us," they said.

I could fully understand and appreciate Cam's exasperation with this Q&A. After all, the odds that anything like this could work in such a large organization would be difficult to grasp. It would be a natural to ask how all this could work without devolving into *Lord of the Flies*–style chaos.

James and I didn't set out to create a nonhierarchical company. It wasn't even on our radar screen in the beginning. We were worried about survival, not titles, reporting relationships, and annual performance reviews.

Over the next years, Menlo grew quickly, and systems, as we had them, seemed to be working out fine. We didn't really question our org chart or our distinctions between bosses and leaders—it just didn't seem important. It really wasn't until Cam asked that fateful question—"Who do people report to here?"—that James and I really started to think about the lack of hierarchy in the organization.

To that point, anytime someone calls us a "bossless" organization, I think James and I would cringe a bit, since we hadn't necessarily set out to become one. James and I developed two canned responses on the topic of hierarchy:

Mine: "Remember, 'bossless' doesn't mean 'leaderless.'"

James: "No, in fact we are ALL bosses here."

But clearly, something had stuck about the no-hierarchy situation, even if it was not deliberate.

James and I wanted to ensure we had a highly adaptive organization to compete in a rapidly changing market. Our customers were asking us to do things that had never been done before, by us, or anyone, for that matter. Designing and implementing a firm hierarchy would have slowed us down.

Our organization was aligned, and we didn't need a formal hierarchy to reinforce that alignment. Our experience is that formal hierarchy usually breeds discord and misalignment as each subhierarchy (departments, divisions, colleges within a university) is pursuing its own unique agenda, often at odds with an organization's mission and stated goals of top leadership.

We were getting strong inputs that our questioning of longstanding corporate traditions was well founded. We were now collecting direct, unbiased evidence—from outside observers, from customers, and internally—that our system was working and working beyond what anyone, including us, could ever have rationally expected.

The need for speed can trump even the best cultural intentions. I believe all of us do things in business for the sake of expediency. We just don't have time to worry about and attend to every little thing as we often have much bigger fish to fry: solve this quarter's revenue targets, get that project out the door, make that next acquisition, hire the next ten staffers, reduce headcount, cut expenses. Hierarchy answers a bunch of questions very quickly—sometimes so quickly that the strength of expediency leads to foundational cultural weaknesses.

Also, hierarchy tends toward fear, no matter how good a person your boss is. The title and office carry weight and intimidating authority. And fear kills even the strongest culture.

As organizations grow, hierarchy can't answer all the questions fast enough without expensively multiplying in breadth and depth. This leads to confusion, which then leads to meeting overload and decision-making slowdown, as information must flow up, across, and down and then back again. In order to expedite this information flow, the hierarchy creates rules so that people can make safe and sanctioned decisions about budgets, activities, conversations, meeting cadence, reporting patterns, and so on. Before you know it, you have full-blown, forms-driven bureaucracy.

Most organizations get here and stay forever, which then leads to the disengagement statistics that just haven't changed much since Gallup started measuring them many years ago. "That's just the way they do things here" becomes the mantra. More and more team members just go through the motions of work and process. They don't even know why, but they learn (or are taught) to never question it.

The good news is that I don't believe an entire hierarchy needs to be dismantled for change to begin and for leadership to replace boss behavior. But you need to ensure that you don't extend the hierarchy—expand it, give it more power—as your leadership culture improves.

Looking back at the changes I made at Interface Systems, it became quite clear that I no longer had any need to multiply the hierarchy to grow. This was a magical moment for me. As VP, it would have been natural to assume that I would need directors, and they would need managers, and they would need group leaders to keep things growing and coordinated. But I found that I needed none of those things—staff engagement was up, energy was up, and the team was self-coordinating and practicing accountability, all without putting in more overhead supervisors. Before my eyes, the team moved faster and faster.

I actually had arguments with my California boss about growing without adding management. He refused to believe the success I was having was anything but luck without my having to add a couple of extra layers of hierarchy. The dot-com explosion left that argument unresolved. The rest would have to be proved out in the months and years ahead at Menlo Innovations.

What does a nonhierarchical system actually look like? It differs from organization to organization, but our version at Menlo breaks down as follows:

We currently have eighteen different pay grades grouped into four categories (Associates, Consultants, Senior, and Principal). Each pay grade is distinct and publicly known by the team both for its pay rate and who at Menlo receives that pay rate. Most newcomers join at the Associate level, our lowest pay grade. Team members advance based on peer evaluation (remember, no bosses to oversee your progress or lack thereof), which often takes the form of Feedback Lunches. If the team determines you are ready to advance and not the whole team but a rational subset of peers, some of your own choosing—they will let you know you are moving up to the next level and you will get a pay increase. Some people advance *very* quickly, others at a slower pace. It is all determined by your peers' assessment of your performance.

Bonuses are paid out based on profits and are shared equally by all team members. We have not created any incentives for you to make yourself look good in comparison to your peers. Rather, just the opposite: *I will do better overall if we all do better.*

This is not a perfect system. Menlo is not for everyone. And we do have standard attrition rates as well. We seldom lose someone we really don't want to, but even that happens. It hurt when Justin, Laura, and Jeff all decided that their weekend trip to Manhattan was so compelling, they were all going to leave around the same time and move to find work in NYC. Ouch. We celebrated their leaving, not because we were glad to see them go; just the opposite. We celebrated this important next stage of their lives.

The absence of a clear hierarchical growth strategy also affects our recruiting. Some need to see upward title mobility or they lose interest. Others who hear about us and indicate employment interest are clearly seeking to plug into what they believe is our existing hierarchy and they want to plug in at a very high level. What all recruits find is a system of advancement that is compelling but vastly different from any they have witnessed before. Some find it refreshing and we become *more* attractive to those candidates. Others are confounded and confused, and some even go so far as to tell us how we should change our existing system to accommodate their needs.

I think a lack of hierarchy enables something magical to happen, though it isn't clear from attrition rates—how we welcome people back to Menlo after they leave. We try to make it clear that valued members of our team may find themselves back in our orbit at some point—and we will greet them with open arms. I can't see this working in a hierarchical organization, where people step on and over one another in fights for promotions, advancements, to be the boss of this or that team. Leaders can plug in and out the way bosses just can't, and that's been an important finding for us.

Tracy B., Menlo mom No. 1 who trailblazed our "babies in the office" experiment, had been a member of our team since the earliest days. In 2002, she left the company when our work slowed. In 2006, she rejoined our team and stayed with us for ten years. When Tracy announced she was leaving us to join a financial services organization in a town north of Ann Arbor, I was sad to see her go, but I think we all knew she was looking for that next exciting personal and professional growth opportunity. We hope she finds it there or somewhere else in the future.

Shortly after leaving, Tracy brought some of her new colleagues for a tour of our offices. Afterward, she stayed on with one of those team members, took up a spot at one of our whiteboard tables, and proceeded to do work as if she were still a member of our team. As the day was coming to a close, I stopped by the table where they were working so intently. I told her how good it was to see her back and jokingly asked her if she still remembered how to lock up if she stayed later than the rest of us.

I don't know if Tracy will ever be back again, but there is a tradition of "Once a Menlonian, always a Menlonian." Tracy isn't the first one to bring her next employer back to Menlo for a tour and visit. She is even suggesting to her employer that they do work with us. Maybe they will, maybe they won't. But that this is even a possibility makes my heart sing. Not for the business but for the relationship and trust it represents. And for the leadership possibilities that exist in this kind of environment.

And beyond trusting relationships there is yet another organizational element that your leaders will need to thrive.

CHAPTER 10

Pursue Systems, Not Bureaucracy

Management's overall aim should be to create a system
in which everybody may take joy in his work.

—Dr. W. Edwards Deming

OUR FIRST DAUGHTER WAS BORN ON MARCH 9, 1984. A FEW WEEKS
later, our whole little family went to see the pediatrician for her
first well-baby checkup. As soon as we stepped into the office, I
realized something was very wrong. There were no other people in
the waiting room.

At the prescribed appointment time, the doctor came out and
asked for Megan Sheridan. I thought that was cute, as Megan was
just a month old. Just then, I noticed that another couple was walking out the door with their child.

We had a wonderful first appointment with our doctor. He taught us how he gave shots without tears. He also taught us that babies move their fingers to every syllable they hear until about a year old, thus it is important to communicate frequently with spoken words. He also taught us to pay attention to how our baby interacted with us and, when she started moving her hands and arms over her head, to know that meant she was in information overload.

For nearly twenty years, the doctor continued to share these types of lessons in every visit with all three of our daughters. I tried hard to never miss an appointment, as I found the whole experience utterly fascinating.

Yet one disturbing constant remained: there were almost never other children in the waiting room. I believed we had stumbled upon one of the most amazing doctors I would ever meet. He was so good in so many ways. So why, I wondered, did he have so few patients? I remembered my own childhood experience with pediatric visits as chaos. A waiting room filled with loads of runny-nosed, coughing children with fevers. Appointments were never on time. In fact, this is still my experience with medical appointments. There was another reason this was disturbing to me: my life at work at the time resembled those chaotic childhood pediatric offices.

One thought haunted me: Was the good doctor just a bad businessman or was this *intentional*? Had he figured something out about creating order and avoiding chaos? I could kind of get how he could do that with planned well-baby checkups, but what about the urgent unplanned visits? There's no way you could predict that, right?

My kids outgrew the pediatric practice and the good doctor eventually retired. I forgot about him and I forgot about those experiences and how they haunted me when I so desperately wanted to escape the mess and chaos of my work life.

In 2013, nearly thirty years after our initial meeting in the good doctor's office, I was working on my first book and I began wondering whatever became of our retired pediatrician. I wondered if he was even still alive. So I Googled "Dr. John Gall."

What came back gives me goose bumps even as I write these words. I quickly learned that Dr. John Gall was not only a wonderful pediatrician and acclaimed professor at the University of Michigan Medical School but also the author of a series of books originally called *The Systems Bible* and later *Systemantics*. Dr. John Gall, it turned out, was one of the world's leading systems thinkers.

Not long after, I went to visit John and his wife, Carol, at their home in Minnesota. I learned what I had always feared: his quiet, empty waiting room was *intentional*. He knew precisely how long his pediatric checkups would take. He knew exactly how many urgent time slots he needed for patients each season and set them aside, so he could always see you the same day if needed. My heart sang to finally learn how important being intentional about your systems and your culture was to creating joy.

Sadly, just a couple months after my visit, on December 15, 2014, John Gall passed away. I was the last visitor they had to their home.

Why should this story be as important to you as it is to me? Because what I have learned over the years is that systems thinking really is critical for developing a bench and culture of great leaders.

When you think about the systems you need in place for your organization to move forward, consider Gall's Law:

"A complex system that works most likely evolved from a simple system that worked. A complex system designed that way from scratch can never be made to work. You must start over with a simple working system."

Systems to Match Your Purpose

Sometimes the bossless aspect of our culture distracts visitors and learners from the more important questions that organizations need to answer to be *intentional* about their culture:

Why do we exist?

Who do we serve?

What would it look like if we could delight the people we serve?

What simple and repeatable processes and methods could we use to systematically produce that delight?

Can we answer the questions above effectively, not just in words but also in everyday actions, while maintaining the spirit and energy of the team doing the work?

I believe any company, any executive, any department, and any organization can answer these questions effectively and productively with or without bosses. Many don't even try.

It's important to consider that while all organizations have a culture, most cultures are *default* cultures defined by the following guidelines:

Whom did we hire? (Evidence of personality-driven organizations)

What behaviors do we tolerate? (Lack of expectation around critical behaviors)

What attitudes walked in the door today? (Lack of trust)

What actions or inactions subtly informed me of what is most important here? (Lack of systems)

These default cultures can work well for a long time until one day they don't, and no one knows why. When a default culture suddenly gets off track, it is impossible to know what could get it back on track. This is because these kinds of cultures are usually driven by the personality of its leaders, not by a worthy purpose. In this environment, if just one personality changes or is pulled out of the equation, the chemistry changes mysteriously.

Intentional cultures thrive when the simple systems put in place reinforce every cultural intention.

If You Want a Culture of Leaders, Build a Culture of Systems Thinkers

After a 2017 talk I gave in Krakow, Poland, one of the attendees pulled me aside to share an important insight based on his experiences. He said leaders who create joyful environments like the one I described in my talk are invariably systems thinkers. This is juxtaposed with those who try to create hero-based cultures that are laden with personality-based antics rather than simple, repeatable, measurable systems.

When things are going poorly within a team or an organization—deadlines being missed, budgets blown, sales targets falling short, quality problems soaring—a leader has a few fundamental choices to consider:

> This is random, and there is nothing we can do but try harder next time.

> If we had better people, these things wouldn't be happening.

> There is something wrong with our system (for sales, scheduling, forecasting, budgeting, quality, etc.).

Systems thinkers will always start with the attitude that improving the systems is the best route to improvement, success, and ultimately joy. Dr. Gall was a great doctor, but it was his system that led to order over chaos.

Imagine the closed-door sessions of many top executives when things aren't going well. How many, in a moment of frustration or business anxiety, aren't tempted to say, "You know, if we only had better people . . . "

This happens all the time in the software industry. We are littered with A-player myth mentality. If quality sucks, the team let us down. It couldn't possibly be that we didn't accurately predict how much work there was before we set the impossible schedule. If the team misses a deadline, it's because they just were not dedicated enough to step up and make it happen. It couldn't possibly be the case that our system to estimate workload was flawed.

The simplest distinction I can make here: Hero-based organizations blame people when things go wrong. System-based organizations ask: "How did our current systems foster these problems?"

Systems-thinkers constantly look for ways to make the "system of work" more humane, more predictable, and able to produce higher quality and foster pride in a team that has the best possible chance to do great work.

One of the best systems we created at Menlo is our time-tracking system. Each week everyone at Menlo (including me) turns in a time sheet accurate down to the quarter of an hour for each task. Time is our most valuable resource, and by tracking our work this way, we can make better predictions about the time needed for any projects we take on in the future. This ensures we don't force people to work crazy overtime, which consequently reduces bugs and helps us avoid the anxiety and loss of morale that always accompanies low-quality work.

Where Do You Start with Systems Thinking?

Here we will start with Albert Einstein: *"Everything should be made as simple as possible, but not simpler."*

There is a very popular version of this quote in the agile software community:

"Do the simplest thing that could possibly work."

By the time we get to high school, we can typically sense the trap in such cleverly worded constructs and start to ask the most obvious question: "How do you know it's the simplest?" and "How do you know you didn't make it too simple?" This is exactly where the leader has to avoid the systems-thinking trap of analysis paralysis:

It may not be the simplest way, but if it is, in fact, simple (in your judgment), go with it.

It may be too simple. Trust you're smart enough to figure that out, go with it for now and adjust later.

This idea of starting with what is simple goes back to Gall's Law. Not all simple systems can stay simple forever; there are always some special cases that will arise. The difference is to not start by anticipating every edge case you can imagine and spend all your time designing the complex system and never getting a chance to start using it. Leaders who think like this and act like this have less to do. Fewer meetings, fewer closed doors and private discussions, less busywork and more real work. The leaders themselves are less burdened and feel more productive. This cascades throughout the team.

We had a small Ann Arbor nonprofit come to visit us and learn about our experiences with allowing parents of newborns to bring their babies to work. They met with me, a couple of the parents, and some team members who had no children just to make sure they were getting a well-rounded view of the implications of such a change within their own organization (they employed fewer than ten people, and they had at least one baby on the way with more likely to follow given the demographic of their staff). I'm guessing they had standard concerns about workplace disruption, unforeseen problems, and an imbalance of enthusiasm for the idea itself within their own team. Standard stuff.

We were happy to spend an hour over lunch with them talking about our experiences. At the time of their visit, we had welcomed more than fifteen Menlo babies in the previous decade (Menlo babies number twenty-one and twenty-two arrived while this book was being written). We are always transparent around this kind of sharing. The babies experiment has been overwhelmingly positive, and we have learned a lot along the way. (Remember this isn't day care . . . the babies are minded by the parents with help from the team.)

It was clear our visitors really appreciated our time and the lessons we shared. I believed they were positively inclined toward trying this out in their own office. Just as we were wrapping up the conversation, one of their team members said:

"Okay, I think our next step is to set up a committee to determine the written policies that should be in place before we begin."

I gently pushed back and, with encouragement, said, "No. Just run the experiment."

I encouraged them to trust their team and try it. If it works, great. If it doesn't, find out what isn't working and adjust. Finally, I offered my experience:

"If you go down the policy-formation route, it will never come out of committee."

We leaders can spend a lifetime planning for the things that never happen and are unprepared to deal with the things, important or otherwise, that come up unexpectedly. We must nurture and grow our ability to actively deal with the very real human things that come up in the day to day. Always trying to hide behind a policy or killing ideas in committee rather than having the difficult conversations will not lead to joy. Honestly, do you think anyone in your organization ever actually reads the policy manual? Do you think they know where to find it? And if every time they try something only to find out later it is "against policy," when will the spirit of "try things" stop?

I am happy to report their first baby arrived and was greeted warmly each Wednesday at the office. Their executive director told me one of the unexpected benefits is that she herself was comforted by holding the baby when facing a challenging decision. Her mental block dissipated when the baby fell asleep in her arms. Joy.

Think back to the story of Amy's team at MassMutual. Amy and her cohort established a culture of experimentation and wanted people to share their ideas. Rather than call IT to build a database of ideas, they bought a tank of helium and balloons. Then they encouraged any employees to go to those desks that were marked with balloons and ask the person at that desk, "What experiment are you running?"

This system was built and functioning at a high level in less than six months inside of the claims division of a 169-year-old insurance company with $30 billion in annual revenues. I dare you to tell me you can't develop a similar attitude of trust in your own organization.

Systems That Reward the Right Behavior

We have a VitalSmarts quote displayed in many places around Menlo. It is a maddening one:

"The systems you have in place are perfectly organized to produce the behaviors you are currently experiencing."

Thus, until we change the systems in such a way as to produce different behaviors, we will experience the common definition of insanity: Keep doing the same thing and expect different results.

Change sticks when your system rewards behavior that you want to see. Many companies get a lot of energy around change initiatives that then peter out as people begin to revert to their old practices. They don't do this because they think the old way is better, necessarily, or because they want to tank the company. They slide because they are not consistently acknowledged and rewarded for doing things the "new, better" way.

Existing rewards systems confound most change efforts. Let's look at how Menlo and other companies have changed reward systems to positively acknowledge the change being sought.

SYSTEMS FOR COLLABORATION

I met Dominique Coster, who runs an R&D team for a worldwide auto supplier, by way of their leader of Human Resources, Suzanne Cislo. Suzanne brought her team, including Dominique, to our offices, to learn about The Menlo Way.

Right from the start I could tell that Dominique was one of the rare leaders who would one day accomplish what he set out to do, which in this case was dramatically shift the culture of the team he was leading in nearby Ypsilanti, Michigan.

What Dominique was pursuing was straightforward. He wished to make the changes necessary to produce the kind of cross-team collaboration he witnessed at Menlo. He engaged us not only to teach but also engaged me directly to do some one-on-one coaching with key leaders who reported to him. It felt a lot like the transformation I had gone through at Interface Systems years before, so I felt comfortable offering advice to this team that had been together a long time. There was clearly willingness and interest in change throughout the organization, so there wasn't much pushback from anyone on the team.

The team began to adapt what they had seen at Menlo. They developed a case study inspired by our recruiting process. They traded the traditional interview for an open and collaborative process where candidates could interact with the entire team in a mutually safe way. They adjusted their office setup to make the space more conducive to spontaneous collaboration and modified some assignments to ensure that teams could cross-pollinate ideas. Within a remarkably short period of time, all the changes they intended to make were in place. Now it was just a matter of time before behaviors would change. Or so we all thought.

I received a call from Dominique a few months later; he was disappointed with their lack of progress. There was no evidence of increased collaboration. I visited again to see for myself and talked again with a few key leaders. I was stymied too. Everything seemed to be in place, including the spirits and attitudes of the team members. Yet, there was no real collaboration.

I then stumbled right into the barrier. "What do you celebrate as a team?" I asked Dominique's team. In particular I asked them what their biggest celebration was. They said *patents*. Patents were very important. Whenever a new patent was issued, the company had a formal celebration. If possible, senior management flew in from Japan to present a plaque to the patent holder in front of the whole team. This was accompanied by a small monetary reward.

I asked what became of the plaques after the ceremony. Dominique's team told me all the plaques are displayed on a wall in the main office corridor. They proudly took me to their Wall of Fame, where, sure enough, dozens of walnut-framed certificates were perfectly arranged, all neatly placed in date order. There was an empty spot at the end that was almost blaring "Your patent goes here!"

I leaned in to take a closer look at each plaque. Each plaque had the patent holder's name neatly embossed on it. Then it hit me.

"This is your problem!" I exclaimed.

"What?" they asked, as if I had called their favorite child ugly.

"You are trying to get to collaboration, yet the single greatest celebration here is for individual achievement. You need to dismantle this reward system, or you will never achieve the results you are seeking."

Soon after, they stopped recognizing only those people who were granted patents and instead began acknowledging the whole team who made that achievement possible. Engineers who worked on product validation and trouble-shooting, accountants, production managers—all those people who contributed were acknowledged and rewarded instead of being left out in the cold. The reward ceremony went from being a more formal affair to a looser and friendlier team occasion.

Note that changing the reward system didn't stop Dominique's team from pursuing patents. The business still needed patents. What they needed more were business innovations, patented or not, that kept them competitive. They needed true collaboration, across engineering disciplines and across departments. Fortunately, they recognized that their existing *systems* were preventing their most ardent desires for change. When they changed their system, they changed their behavior.

The new collaborative style that resulted from this simple system change means that there might be two or three names on a patent instead of just one. The reward system, now focused on team contribution rather than individual accomplishment, makes this a serious possibility. It works for the business and for the team. These kind of simple system changes can also provide fertile ground for developing new leaders, as these team members who formerly were waiting their turn for the limelight now work shoulder-to-shoulder with seasoned leaders who are no longer worrying about keeping rewards to themselves.

SYSTEMS FOR TRANSPARENCY

One of the biggest challenges in an endeavor as theoretical as software development is that there is almost no way to ascertain true progress from a status report. If you are an executive and your software team tells you they are 60 percent done, how would you be certain of what that means exactly? What confidence would you have in the simple math represented by that number?

The most common lament about software projects is that it takes the first 90 percent of the budget to get the first 90 percent done and it takes the second 90 percent of the budget to get the last 10 percent done. In this joke, however, is a lot of human pain. When budgets are blown and deadlines missed, heads roll, overtime is mandated, and projects are eventually cancelled. This happens way more often than most people realize.

The next level of challenge is even if your team gets to "done" and the product is finished, someone is very likely going to say, "But that's not what we asked for." More heads roll, more overtime for the rework, and more cancellations.

Usually by the time anything gets out the door, it is a shadow of what was originally desired, the team is glad to be done with it, and there is little to celebrate. Not much reward here. In fact, the greatest reward is typically "I get to keep my job."

In the Java Factory at Interface Systems, we met this challenge head on with a Show and Tell every two weeks. We invited the key business stakeholders to the meeting to ensure the people who were counting the most on our results could see what we were accomplishing.

At these biweekly events, we would put together a simple theater with chairs all lined up, a computer and projector at the front of the room, and a pull-up movie screen. The stakeholders were assembled in the audience: salespeople hoping to see our newly conceived products, product managers who directed our efforts toward what they believed the market was telling them, executives who were authorizing the funding for these various efforts, and the occasional board member.

James and I saw this as an important opportunity to bind the relationship between the technical team and the business units. This was a relationship often marked by missed deadlines and less-than-stellar results. Phrases like "We are done, but we aren't done-done" would just frustrate the relationship between technologists and management.

Each one of these Show and Tell sessions concluded with a variety of questions from the stakeholder attendees. The questions were pointed and interesting. My team sensed excitement because for the first time ever, they saw that people in the rest of the company really cared about their progress and were counting on product improvements that could increase sales and answer real client needs.

Word spread throughout the company about the Show and Tells. Others began showing up just to see what was going on. Still others wondered if they could come see. Even Marie, the receptionist, came to see the hoopla. She said for the first time she understood what our company did for our customers. My team's energy rose as the audience expanded.

To increase energy, enthusiasm, and participation, my team started to bring little hard candies to Show and Tell. Each time a question was asked, a candy was thrown out to the audience member. Every cycle brought new ideas as to how to make the presentation even more compelling.

Show and Tells were now a must-see event. They continue to this day at Menlo, for each cycle, for each customer. We eventually switched the presenter role to our customer to bring full engagement from the people who are paying us to do the work. Yes, at Menlo Show and Tells, our customers show *us* our work while the team who did the work watches with enthusiasm to see how their hard work is received by the person who cares the most: our customer.

The reward for the team in this case is the regular feedback they are getting on their work. Even if someone is complaining that something isn't working the way they are expecting, there is still time to work on it without huge fanfare. The technical team gets excited about their work because the people relying on their work are getting excited about what has been accomplished. They feel as though their efforts are appreciated and valued and that they matter.

There is an emcee role for Show and Tells, and at Menlo we do this in pairs (of course). As different team members are asked to emcee each Show and Tell, they are able to stretch their leadership wings and experiment with ways to make the public presentations to our clients more compelling, which is a reward in and of itself.

This simple system, which fosters short communication and feedback loops, without hierarchy or bureaucracy fuels the human energy of the team.

SYSTEMS AVOID FINGER-POINTING

James, in the earliest days of Menlo, told the team, "I am the leader of operations, so if something goes wrong, blame me. Tell everyone it's my fault."

One particularly difficult day on a tough project where something wasn't working right, Ted, one of our longtime team members and a leader in his own right, caught the team trying to pinpoint fault for the problem in question. Ted sensed the leadership moment in this challenging conversation and declared: "It's James's fault. Now let's go solve the problem."

It worked! The team took all their attention away from fault-finding and got down to the far more important task at hand. This became a team mantra from this day forward and did a lot to quell fear within the team. If we can quickly establish fault, especially with a cofounder whom we cannot hunt down and wound, we can spend our time much more productively finding and solving problems, which is what an engineering team like ours enjoys doing anyway.

If we declare we have a blame-free culture, we are kidding ourselves. Finding the culprit when something doesn't work well enough to succeed is a time-honored human tradition. When it's a big enough catastrophe, we will assemble a government panel and produce a thousand-page report that will be archived in the Library of Congress or some other national archive.

We are not expecting perfection. We acknowledge that we are first and foremost human. People make mistakes. Every. Single. Day. Keep these mistakes small enough, provide an obvious scapegoat, and fear begins to leave the room.

This is evidence of systems thinking at work. Having a built-in response when things are going wrong diffuses tensions quickly and is a beautiful structure to getting back to work.

Another version of automated responses at Menlo is "Rich is uncomfortable!" when anyone says or does something that feels inappropriate in a professional work environment. This phrase entered our lexicon in the earliest days of Menlo, when someone made an inappropriate comment, likely steeped in innuendo, and I could feel the tension in our tiny storefront office. Leaning on my sense of humor to diffuse the tension, I called out "Well *that* makes me uncomfortable," and it broke the tension with a big roar of laughter. I invoked this a couple more times in the coming months to ensure people knew I wasn't going to ignore inappropriate behavior. My recollection is that the behaviors I was calling out were nowhere near the lines being crossed in so many workplaces we read about these days in the news. If these were movie-rating moments, the worst cases were PG-13. At some point, the team picked up on this and started filling in for me (even when I was there) by calling out "Rich is uncomfortable!" It gets a strong laugh every time and we get back to work.

Not all systems need to be complex processes—we have verbal cues that help us respond to problems that might arise and get back to work. There are numerous sayings—some important enough to print on colorful posters—we have at Menlo that basically function as simple systems: they steer us away from chaos and toward order. Any person in the organization can employ these, which include the following:

"Run the Experiment"

"Make Mistaks Fatser" (a slight improvement on the Java Factory's *Make Mistakes Faster*)

"It's OK to say 'I don't know.'"

"Fear doesn't make bad news go away. Fear makes bad news go into hiding."

"An example right about now would be really helpful."

"Make your partner look good."

"Look for good kindergarten skills."

"Dolphin-speak" (an encouragement to our technologists to curb the geek-speak)

"What problem are we trying to solve?"

"Let's drop that idea in the Solution bucket." (Used when we start coming up with solutions long before we understand the problem we are trying to solve; FYI: We actually have little red buckets with a label that says *Solution Bucket*.")

Is there a story card for that? (Our way of avoiding hallway project management. Of course, we don't have any hallways either! ☺)

All these little things we do help foster a system that keeps us feeling safe, productive, and energized without bureaucracy or a need to call a meeting. These simple constructs also provide new leaders some basic constructs from which to develop their own leadership style. There are many more, but those listed are among our most commonly used.

A SYSTEM FOR SPEAKING TRUTH TO POWER

About three times a year, we schedule what we affectionately refer to as a quarterly meeting. We gather the whole team for a few hours to discuss the state of the business and then spend most of our time answering questions that are on the team's mind. The questions are often submitted ahead of time so we can keep the discussion on track and allow the team to both hear about the things of greatest interest and get home to their families on time. It also means the team sets the agenda, not James and me. We don't worry about deep preparation for such gatherings, as the goal is to be open, authentic, and vulnerable.

I know that regardless of how strong a culture of leaders we build, James and I, as co-owners, will still be seen as the power in the company. And we can't successfully run or grow the business unless we are to openly discuss the hard truths about what is going on at any given moment. James and I have a responsibility to the team to allow this to happen and for everyone to be safe in doing so.

Our October 2017 quarterly meeting fell right in the middle of our "state of fear," and the collective mood was reflected in the tough questions James and I fielded that evening. I had been traveling most of the ten days leading up to the day of the meeting, so there would be no time to prepare.

Here's a sampling of what Lisa, Michelle, and Emily threw our way for that evening's meeting: I've added some commentary [in brackets] for color.

We have asked the team to submit their questions for tomorrow's meeting, which are listed below. We wanted to give them to you ahead of time so you can be prepared to respond. [James and I didn't have time to prepare for this particular meeting due to other priorities, but having the questions written down ahead of time gave the team time to prepare their thoughts for us.] *Some of us feel that in the past we haven't always gotten direct, actionable responses from you, and we would look for that from you in tomorrow's meeting.* [Ouch; talk about important feedback.]

As you know, Menlo has continued to go through many changes the last few years and has faced some financial challenges a couple of times during this period. The questions below are a direct result of how the team is feeling and where their concerns lie as it pertains to the changes the business has gone or is going through:

It feels like FOOBB [note: this is our Financial Operations Open Book Board meeting, which happens every Monday at 3:00 p.m., with the whole team] *is only creating fear in the team, rather than actionable items that can be made to improve the business. What is the current value of running FOOBB? What are your goals for FOOBB?* [Great question and one of the leadership questions to which James and I shouldn't just respond "Because we said so!"]

Are you concerned about the number of developers that have been leaving Menlo lately? What are some action items Menlo could address to prevent loss of more team members? [Yup. I hate it too.]

How do we stay competitive when we pay much less than our competitors? If it's culture, how do we help grow that? [But we are *Joy, Inc.,* for goodness' sake.]

Most people that work at Menlo take a pay cut to work here because they value other things that Menlo has to offer. It feels like the intangible benefits that used to make us so excited to work here and willing to take a pay cut are less than they used to be. [It is not our goal to pay less, but a strong adherence to a forty-hour workweek does change our financial equation. The second half of the question is far more important.]

With respect to sales, do we have the right people in the right roles? Do we need an outside perspective to help us? We know this is something that was not successful in the past, but that was one experience, maybe something that should be revisited? How should we be focusing on sales? What experiments can we run? How can we be more proactive rather than reactive? How can we be more consistent week to week focusing on sales? [Evidence of leadership and a desire to lead from the team, not just looking to James and me to have all the answers.]

Would you consider working with a business consultant to help us with business strategy? [The team is asking James and me to consider that we may need some professional growth.]

How are we changing and adjusting to our competition and the changes in types of people/companies coming through the door and what they are looking for?

We believe we saw the "October cliff" back in July/August. It feels like we did very little to try and prevent going over the cliff. What do you think we should have done differently?

What are 2018 goals? What is your strategy for reaching 2018 goals?

In what ways has our culture changed in the last year? Which of these changes are the most beneficial and which are the most problematic? (From your perspective.)

It was a good and important discussion that evening. I reminded the team that James and I are open to trying many things. We are just as willing as anyone to run new experiments to solve these problems. We aren't heroes, though. We are a team first and foremost, and our ability to come together as a team will define our ability to overcome the challenges we face.

As Patrick Lenicioni says in the opening line of *Five Dysfunctions of a Team*: "Not finance. Not strategy. Not technology. It is teamwork alone that is the ultimate advantage, both because it is so powerful and so rare."*

Now, some may be reading the questions above and thinking, "Whoa, it doesn't sound like *Joy, Inc.* to me." It certainly didn't feel that way to me in the moment, either. Yet it was the team strength and trust we had for each other that made such questions fair game

* Patrick Lenicioni, *Five Dysfunctions of a Team: A Leadership Fable* (Hoboken, NJ: Jossey-Bass, 2002).

in such an open setting. Did I feel vulnerable? Sure. Afraid? No way. The very fact that our team was willing to explore their greatest fears in a group setting and speak those fears to James and me will remain one of our key strengths as an organization.

Our long-standing pattern of quarterly meetings means there is an established system for a group exploration of important topics. Newer team members participate fully yet also watch and learn that asking challenging questions is not frowned upon. Our seasoned leaders are modeling behavior. The discussions are always respectful.

I sent a thank you to Lisa a few weeks later telling her that I so appreciated her willingness to walk alongside me and the Menlo team as we figure out our best future together. Knowing her strong faith walk, I asked for her continued prayers.

She replied: "I am very energized and excited by all the experiments and creativity going on right now. Thank you for how you've been listening to the team over the past weeks and for all the ideas and experiments you have initiated. God is good, and we have many things to be thankful for this holiday season."

Joy.

Taking Care of Each Other

We must remember as well that our team and our leaders are regular people and must be taken care of and not taken for granted. This is a system too; one we take very seriously.

CHAPTER 11

Care for the Team

I worry that business leaders are more interested in material gain than they are in having the patience to build up a strong organization, and a strong organization starts with caring for their people.

—John Wooden

WE HAVE A UNIQUE WAY OF BRINGING NEW PEOPLE ON TO OUR team. Essentially, we look for applicants to express passion for our work style or show an understanding of our story in their cover letters. If we see evidence of interest and fit, we invite them to participate in our Extreme Interviewing process, which is basically a mass audition for employment.

The first audition gathers as many as fifty candidates in a room together. We ask them to complete three twenty-minute exercises done in pairs, with another candidate who is interviewing for the same position. A Menlonian is assigned to watch each unique pairing and take notes. They look past how well they execute the assignment and focus instead on how well they collaborate. In fact, we tell each candidate that their job is to "make your partner look good"—to help the stranger sitting next to them get a shot at a second interview. We then switch the pairs for two other rounds before doing a wrap-up Q&A and sending everyone home.

This open audition can cast a wide net, and the catch we pull in might seem unusual for a software company: housekeeping managers; waitresses; landscapers; welders; criminal justice majors; anthropologists; PhDs in astronomy, genetics, biology. We will give them all a good look on the first try, to see how well they pass the kindergarten skills test: "Do they play well with others?"

At the end of the first round of interviews, our team gathers to discuss each candidate and decides whom they want to bring in for a second round of interviews.

The next stage of the interviewing process involves doing real work, paired alongside two different Menlo employees over the course of a day. This is a paid day—we give you a one-day stipend to work on a real project. At this point, we are checking more concretely for skills such as programming ability, design aptitude, or project management instincts depending on the role they are seeking. Skills matter, of course, but failing "fit for culture" trumps all other qualifications. It is one of the most important things we can do to safeguard the ecosystem we have created.

After the one-day trial, the Menlonians who were paired with the candidate discuss how they performed. Did the candidate do the work? Would they want to pair with this person again? If it's a yes on all fronts, we offer the candidate a three-week paid trial. During this time, they pair with at least three other Menlonians and do real, move-the-ball-forward work on client projects with us. At the end of the three-week trial, if all goes well and we mutually decide it is a good fit—we officially have a new Menlonian. It's a great cause for celebration.

Our interview is very inclusive on the Menlo side as well. Even if you've only been with us a few weeks, are an intern, and/or just graduated from college, you are encouraged to volunteer to be an observer at our interviews. Too often, interviewing in many companies is reserved for the big dogs and the seasoned veterans. Here, your vote and your voice have equal weight in the follow-on discussion. What better way to plant seeds for leadership development?

This process is interesting and flawed. Despite its flaws, though, it is better than any alternative we've seen elsewhere or used in our previous work lives. Still, we do miss good people along the way and sometimes mistakenly bring in poor fits. The latter is sorted out later with some pain.

A Culture of Leadership Invests in People

Scott K. fell into the "miss good people" category. He really wanted to work for us, interviewed with us, and we turned him down. He was persistent and tried again a year later, getting through the first round. He also passed the second round, the one-day paid trial where candidates pair with two different Menlonians to actually work on a project.

Scott's educational background was in welding, not software. Yet, he spent his spare time teaching himself programming as he found passion there. Since we don't look at résumés when we interview, we are able to take chances on people who wouldn't normally pass the résumé-sorting process. Scott appreciated that we weren't automatically disqualifying him based on a sheet of paper.

Sadly, Scott failed the third round three-week paid trial with our team. He really wanted to succeed, but he was not able to adjust his behavior based on the team's comments. We wanted Scott to succeed, and as much as Scott wanted to as well, he didn't. The major problem was that Scott struggled with thinking out loud, an important requirement for effective pairing. After three weeks of constructive criticism and encouragement, we talked to Scott and let him know it just wasn't working. He was sad and so were we.

The team decided, though, that there was enough there to give it one more try with Scott. In an unusual move, they said they would press the reset button on his three-week paid trial and give him another three weeks. The team told Scott they would double down their feedback efforts and Scott would match it with his own desire to improve. But after week four, he still wasn't lining up.

On week five, Scott was paired with David M., a slender, gentle giant of a programmer. Scott pulled David aside and said, "Look, I'm failing and I don't want to fail. I need something more from the process we are using. It's not working for me."

Our typical style was to give feedback at the end of each day and again at the end of each week. Scott asked for direct and pointed comments right in the moment and David agreed to try it, even though he found this request uncomfortable as he had only been with us for a couple of months and wasn't yet used to giving direct, critical feedback.

This slight modification was all the magic Scott needed. Every time he stopped thinking out loud, David would stop him and say, "Scott you're doing it again!" Scott adapted quickly as he simply started thinking out loud.

Scott's performance totally changed, and he has become a valued member of our team. Our team loves him and so do our customers. I expect he will rapidly be recognized as a strong and valued leader. Leaning into authenticity—being vulnerable in front of others, believing your whole self is a worthy self to share with others—has never failed us. Neither has understanding our accountability to one another.

While this is a story about Scott, it is also a story about David M. and the leadership he showed in his commitment to help Scott succeed. It is also a story about the team's willingness to take a chance on Scott when it would have been easy to just move on to the next candidate and find someone more immediately suitable for our team and our culture.

I believe this emanates from the authentic relationships we build with each other every single day by working so closely together. While our work style and environment may not be suitable or palatable to many, there must be a concerted effort for building relationships around the work itself. Meetings, pep talks, company picnics, and lunchrooms won't always be enough.

Building in Caring

If you want to establish "caring for each other" in your own organization, I would recommend you look at every "people" system you have in place today and consider what changes you might make.

For us, evidence of our caring is exhibited first during the interview. Within a few minutes of arriving at our Extreme Interview event, candidates hear instructions that portend our caring intention:

"Make your pair partner look good."

"Help the person sitting next to you get a second interview." (Even though they are competing for the same position you are.)

"If your partner is struggling, help them out."

"If your partner is nervous, try to set them at ease."

"Don't grab the pencil out of their hands."

"Demonstrate good kindergarten skills. Play well with others. Share."

After two hours of watching these exercises play out among their potential future peers, the Menlonians who watched them gather over food and discuss what they saw.

This open discussion about each and every individual who

attended the event lasts for two or three hours, depending on how many candidates attended. This is one of the most heartfelt discussions we have about our core values as we explore what made each individual special and interesting to our team. The decision point isn't whether to hire but rather did we see enough evidence of good kindergarten skills to invite them in for a second interview?

Onboarding Is a Make-or-Break Point

What was your first day like where you work? Was it all forms and bureaucracy or was there evidence of a team who cares about your success?

Most people I talk to describe the first day on a job as one of the more difficult and uncomfortable experiences they have with a new employer. It often feels like your arrival was somehow unexpected.

We treat our second interview as your first day of work on the new job. You spend a day with us, you do work with us, and we pay you for this work. We assign a Menlonian to greet you and pair with you for the morning. You'll go out to lunch with the team, so you have a chance to meet other people on the team and they you. In the afternoon you are paired with another Menlonian to get a different experience with our work. At the end of the day, one or two other Menlonians check in with you, make sure you've filled out the forms that allow you to get paid and ask you how your day went and answer any additional questions you have.

If the day went well for you, and us, we invite you back for a three-week paid trial, like the one described above with Scott.

I would encourage you to notice and think about one other important element of our entire process for interviewing and hiring: It is *success* oriented. We want and expect the candidate to succeed and we will do everything in our power to make that happen. Most interview processes I've heard about elsewhere are doing what they can to disqualify candidates. This negative approach sets the stage for a culture that learns to continue this pattern of disqualification at every stage of the employment journey. Raises are "hard to get," promotions must be fought over, and annual performance review ratings ensure that most only "meet expectations" no matter how hard you try. The worst version of this played out at large companies that implemented a "cut the lowest 10 percent of performers every year." It is little wonder that "fixed mind-sets" pervade so many companies leading many of their employees to conclude, "The only way I can get ahead is to leave."

Avoid Hero Worship

The software industry is like so many others, built on the shoulders of heroes. The A-player myth is a strong one in business but comes at such a high cost, even for the hero.

Michael Jordan was beyond any measure an A player in the world of pro basketball. Yet, between 1987 and 1990, the Chicago Bulls weren't winning championships. They could not get by the Detroit Pistons in the playoffs. Phil Jackson was installed as head coach and, as a true developer of leaders, had to teach his A player to be part of the team rather than the hero. He needed Michael to lead. For Michael to lead, he had to start caring deeply about the development of the other members of the team. They needed to play a role in the success of the team and play a much bigger role in winning games, especially the tough ones. It would be important for the Bulls *team* to hear the cheers, not just Michael.

Watching hero Michael Jordan was fun, unless you were a Bulls fan who thought that championship rings were the true measure of success. Once Michael became part of the team, they started winning. Michael became a leader on the court, no longer the individual hero. He didn't back off his skills, his contributions, his practice ethic; he added leadership to his talents, and they started winning.

For Coach Jackson, Jordan's defining moment came during the team's first championship run in 1991 (the first of six). Speaking about the change in Michael's stepping back from "hero" to on-court leader, Jackson said:

"That was the defining moment, his transition from being a great scorer to learning how to beat teams without having to score. He knew we'd win *championships* because of it. It was a changing moment for him."*

Our team is filled with such an interesting collection of team players. Some don't have a high school diploma. Several have PhDs in fields as diverse as anthropology, genetics, and astronomy. Each individual makes amazing and highly valued contributions and they know each other so well, they know exactly who to turn to when a specific challenge is vexing us.

---

* "Phil Jackson: Michael Jordan's Contributions Will Never Be Eclipsed," https://www.nba.com/bulls/news/jordanhof_jackson_090827.html.

Where we excel is our ability to work on challenges together and work them out together. Mostly. There are very few times where intervention is required, and when it is required from James or me, we try to do so gingerly to give the team the space to continue to grow and work on things for not only personal growth but also team growth.

What we must avoid is the temptation to elevate the heroes. Do it just once and you will quickly change to a hero-based environment.

I once called "Hey, Menlo" during a tour and praised a single team member for their "heroic efforts" solving a business problem over the weekend. I asked the team to applaud the person, noting that their individual contribution made all the difference in solving a complex problem. The team tepidly started clapping, trying to look into my eyes from across the room to see if I was serious. I wasn't—I had made up the story in jest, to see their reaction.

After a minute of confused clapping, one team member spoke up: "Hey, we don't do that here!"

"Too true," I agreed. We all had a great laugh together and got back to work.

If we speak of teamwork, yet reward individual heroes with praise and promotions, we implicitly develop a system of heroic leaders. That can work until the leader stumbles, and those around them silently cheer so that they can get their turn in the spotlight.

We want our entire team to care deeply about their leaders and if they stumble to be right there to help them up.

Care Enough to Let the Team Build the Team

I meet with a lot of students, entrepreneurs, and other folks in the Ann Arbor area, to grab a cup of coffee and chat about business. As you might imagine, some of these conversations turn into discussions about a desire to join our team. I am always flattered when that happens.

You might imagine their surprise when they learn that the CEO, cofounder and co-owner of the company tells them that I have nothing to do with who joins our team. I can certainly ensure they are invited to our next Extreme Interview (I do have *that* much influence), but I let them know that our team builds the team. I also have little influence on promotions or feedback lunches, unless I work directly with someone on the team. After all, these peers will, at some point, sit by your side and collaborate with you for a forty-hour workweek. It would be unusual for me to have a better or more valid opinion than those who must work side by side with you or who will face our customers in Show and Tells when presenting the results of the work we've done together.

While these coffee conversations might turn into a moment of disappointment when people realize that connecting with the CEO for a brief time did not produce the advantage they were seeking, I remind them that their long-term success at Menlo will only be assured if the team adopts them.

In this way, I am caring for our leaders by saying, I trust you and will not undermine you at the most important junctures.

Take a Chance on People

One of the guiding principles mentioned in the introduction was "Take a chance on people." This was certainly the case with Brian, who passed the culture fit test of the Extreme Interview with flying colors but quickly demonstrated a lack of technical prowess— nearly the opposite of Scott's situation.

Brian came in for his one-day trial and paired with Adam in the morning and Scott in the afternoon on the Starbird project, a comprehensive business application for a national retailer using Amazon Web Services. He was likely already feeling the pressure of technical gaps during this one day of working at Menlo. He made it through, but perhaps *not* with flying colors this time, as the learning curve was steep for this project. Yet, there were another two thumbs-up (and a third from Brian himself). The team decided to extend to him an invitation for a three-week paid trial.

His three-week trial successfully exposed his lack of deep technical skills. In my old life, Brian likely would not have made it this far without some clever manipulation of the interview process, but even if he squeaked through my old traditional interview process, the experience of the technical trial would have smoked him out for lacking the exact and perfect skills needed to join my old team.

Yet, the Menlo team saw something in him they liked. Brian had a calm maturity, a deep desire to be a humble learner, and a focus on helping his partners succeed. The team encouraged him to take books home and study up on Agile, Java, and other software techniques and tools. After three weeks, when we usually have a clear decision point, the team was conflicted. They loved him as a Menlonian but knew he didn't have the programming chops to be a valued technical contributor. They did see learning. Just not enough.

They gave him an extended shot. They told him they wanted him to stay around for an eight-week trial if he was game. He was. As these are all team decisions, I had no idea this was going on.

Late in his seventh week, Brian came to standup with a red folder containing some papers. When the Viking helmet got to him, he said:

"Good morning, I'm Brian, and as many of you know I am in the seventh week of my eight-week trial. Since I don't know whether I make it or not after week eight, I want to gather feedback about my progress, so even if you let me go, I'll know what I need to work on, and hopefully improve enough to come back. So I put together a form with three columns, 'What is going well? What isn't? Actions to take.' I will pass this out directly to people I've worked with, but if anyone else has something to add, I have this red folder with extra copies. I'd really appreciate your feedback."

Holy cow. Here was a guy saying to the team and visitors (as we had some visitors in that day attending standup): "I don't know if I'm being fired next week or not, but I'm eager to get feedback regardless."

Brian had a team feedback session at the end of the eight-week trial period. He mentioned that even he wasn't sure if he is bringing enough value for the owners to hire him. Kealy reminded him that this was a team decision and that the owners were not weighing in. (I did appreciate his recognition of connecting a paying job to value delivered to those paying him.)

The team placed a bet on Brian and invited him to stay. They brought him in at a pay level below our typical Associate I entry level. Again, their choice, and Brian had to be OK with that. He was.

I believe this is a perfect story for enunciating our belief in taking a chance on people. It won't just be up to Brian to come up to the speed we need. The team, now that the bet has been placed, is also committed to helping him succeed. Brian will also have his work cut out for him. Nothing is certain in the path forward. Yet, if we look back a few years from now and see not only a team member who pulled himself up to compete on the stage of Menlo, I'm sure we will have also cultivated a leader who himself will remember this time and be one of those willing to place a bet and then do the other side of work to help ensure the bet pays off.

Caring for our leaders means extending that caring in their earliest days at the company, before they are leaders, so that they know exactly what caring looks and feels like from a very personal perspective.

Caring through Consistent Feedback

During 2015 and 2016 I was out of the office a lot, traveling around the world to speak with companies about joy in the workplace. After returning from one trip, while seated at my table checking email, I heard someone sing out (literally sing) *"Feedbackies!"* (If you recall the *Green Giant* commercials, that's what this little jingle sounded like).

I turned my head to see what the heck was going and didn't see much difference in the Factory cadence. Each pair was talking to one another, so nothing unusual there.

Since Corey was the one who had sung out the word, I went over and asked what was going on. He said they were doing 4:45 p.m. "Feedbackies." Huh?

He explained to me that the team realized that they still kind of sucked at giving each other critical feedback. It was uncomfortable and if they waited until the end of the week—or worse, until the next Feedback Lunch, which could be months away—it would really be hard to give helpful, yet critical feedback.

The team decided they needed to practice this skill a few minutes every day. So "Feedbackies" was born. Over time, pairs established a pattern of asking each other "How did I do today?" to remove the tension that came with the other person having to open up an awkward conversation.

This daily routine, which ran for a few months, gave our team a chance to practice a rather uncomfortable skill. Framed as a caring exercise, though, this activity wasn't met with trepidation or fear but open-mindedness and maybe even a little bit of fun. It allowed us to build skills when the stakes were low, so they'd be more readily available to us when the stakes were high.

Tough Love

Menlo is not all rainbows and unicorns. Like everyone else, we have hard people issues to work on. It could be attendance or performance or being a good pair partner. And sometimes life just gets in the way of allowing a person to be their best self at work.

When these perfectly natural issues come up, a team that cares for itself must ask: Do we say something or let it ride? If we say something, can we do so with compassion and understanding? If tough love is required, can it be delivered in a way that isn't harsh?

I think this is the most difficult part of building a team that knows how to care for itself. It is so easy to look the other way and assume the situation will either take care of itself, or someone else will handle it. In our environment, this is compounded by the fact that no one has a boss who is specifically charged with watching after this.

Our saving grace in holding each other accountable happens first in the pairs and the fact that the pairs switch often. It is much harder in such an environment to slide by for a long time. However, the questions still arise. If one pair partner notices some challenges, do they say something to the person? Do they raise this concern with their peers?

"Caring" can sometimes feel harsh or downright cruel if the only thing a struggling team member is hearing about is "accountability" and "performance." This is especially true if the struggles emanate from something happening outside of work, like medical problems or struggles in their family lives. This is why we teach Menlonians to ask, "Are you okay?" We need to care about the person, the whole person, and not just the employee.

I can recall two team members who over the years had both struggled with attendance issues, related to personal struggles outside of work. The team wrestled with how to address both cases. Ultimately they responded with thoughtful solutions that likely saved both from eventual firing. In one case, a team member stepped up on behalf of the other telling that staff member, "If you are about to send an 'out' message on any given morning, call my cell just before you press Send and tell me what is going on."

In another case, a team member volunteered to pick the employee up every morning at their home and bring them to work. In both instances, attendance improved dramatically.

Sometimes feedback does not produce the desired results and a decision is made to terminate a staff member. In this case, I personally coach the team when delivering the news, that the discussion must immediately shift from "Bill the employee with performance challenges" to "Bill the person." I ask them what "Bill" will need more than anything in this moment. In some cases, it's a shot at another job. If so, I tell them to send "Bill" to me and I can open my personal network to him. Sometimes the person who is being asked to leave wants to know they are still going to be friends with our team; they want to know that our social system is still available to them. In one case, we invited a team member to a future standup so they could say a proper goodbye. It was very touching and included hugs all around. Just so we are clear, though, it doesn't always go this well. For some, the parting is just too painful, or we weren't at our best when we delivered the news.

This tough love aspect of our culture may be the most important aspect of the care and feeding of our team. It is also the hardest part of building a great team and culture of leaders. If we always look the other way during performance challenges, the overall morale will drop as some who are carrying their own weight will wonder why they also have to carry the weight of those who are underperforming. We all carry a strong sense of fairness in our souls that must be honored.

If we don't care enough to give tough feedback to each other, it is often the case that the leaders end up carrying the majority of the extra burden brought on by low performers. Thus, caring for our leaders means being tough on obvious performance challenges.

I will use a specific challenge in these kind of circumstances by asking "Why do we care so little for 'Bill' that we wouldn't want to share critical feedback?" When the team responds that we don't want to hurt "Bill's" feelings, I ask them how much more it will hurt Bill when we fire him a few weeks from now.

A newer team member was really struggling to pair well with one of our best leaders. The new employee needed a different kind of support than was being offered but didn't feel safe bringing it up given the imbalance in seniority. Ian noticed and intervened. He led both team members to have an honest conversation that became a bit emotional. The dialogue produced great results and healed the relationship from that point forward.

Looking out for the whole person can manifest itself in so many ways. Here are some other ways our team has demonstrated deep caring for each other:

Chris H. announces around the holidays every year that anyone who does not have a place to go at Thanksgiving or Christmas is automatically invited to spend it with his family.

Eric S. opened his home to Seth's family while Seth was looking for a house during his relocation to Michigan.

Kealy became aware of a longtime team member struggling with depression and invited that team member to join her and her husband on their summer vacation in northern Michigan. She later arranged dinners for the three of them during the year.

Renee designed all the paper materials for both Kealy's and Anna's weddings.

We opened the Menlo office one evening for a team member's family friends, who needed a neutral space to work through family discord on the heels of a loss. Being in a neutral space allowed them to set aside their differences for an evening and focus on the memory of their loved one.

They don't only care for one another. They care for me too.

Anna coordinates my life so wonderfully while working with the outside world for my speaking, traveling, and company visits. In 2015, I gave forty-four talks around the world. I enjoy the work and meeting new people, but it may have been just too much. Before I could articulate that, Anna was already on it. She told me she was turning down all requests for me to travel anywhere in December of that year. "You need to make sure you have time with your family, Rich," she told me.

The following February, Carol and I traveled with our whole family to the Caribbean for a delightful mid-winter vacation. As I was squeezing everything in before I left, Anna reminded me of an expectation we have for all our team members: "You know Rich, you need to really enjoy this vacation. I don't think you should check email while you are away."

I froze as I contemplated the paradox of her suggestion. I knew she was right, but I also knew I didn't want to come home to a jammed in-box full of a thousand messages to sort through on the first day back.

"I can take care of your email. I'll save the ones only you can handle and let them know you're on vacation," she said.

With some trepidation, we ran the experiment. I moved the email icon off the home screen of my phone so I wouldn't be tempted. When I returned home, Anna had handled all but eighteen of my messages. I was caught up on my email by 9:00 a.m. the morning I returned.

That's caring for your team. And that's joy.

Our focus is to develop an entire culture of caring, and not specifically caring *by* leaders or even *for* leaders. However, by choosing to require caring from our leaders, we must provide a fertile environment for equipping our staff to grow into the role of being a caring leader. Everyone at Menlo must develop this ability to care for others. It is only in this practice of caring that our leadership corps will grow into this great, and quite frankly, challenging territory.

This is one of those areas we must never be satisfied. There will always be room for improvement. There will always be room for *learning*.

CHAPTER 12

Learn Together

The illiterate of the twenty-first century will not be those who cannot read and write, but those who cannot learn, unlearn and relearn.

—Alvin Toffler

I AM GOING TO ASSERT SOMETHING ABOUT YOUR ORGANIZATION, even though I don't know you or your company. You are currently facing an existential threat from a competitor, a technology, or an industry that didn't even exist or have a name when your company was founded.

Borders Books was put out of business by a website. The company was founded in 1971 by Tom and Lou Borders in a storefront on State Street in Ann Arbor, Michigan. The first web browser wouldn't hit the market until 1994; Amazon was founded in July of that year. In 2011, its final year, Borders employed 19,500 people throughout the United States.

Borders had seventeen years to learn how to adapt to the changing landscape. They couldn't. They didn't. They disappeared.

This type of disruption is evident throughout human history. What is different now is the pace of change. We can't prepare our organizations to succeed in such a rapid change environment unless we productively rekindle our curiosity and reawaken the able learners inside of all of us. Our leaders and aspiring leaders must be active learners. Whatever we studied or learned decades ago may lay a foundation for our work today, but we must continually adapt or will we also disappear.

One of the books that started me on my journey back to joy was Peter Senge's *The Fifth Discipline: The Art & Practice of the Learning Organization*. One of the oft-quoted lines from that book states the problem so well for all of us: "In the long run, the only sustainable source of competitive advantage is your organization's ability to learn faster than your competition."*

If learning is key to survival, then it must be present in our systems and our regular activities. We must, for example, shorten our communication and feedback loops. If a feedback loop is too long, it will either have no effect or worse, the opposite of the intended effect. For example, consider the negative effect of annual performance reviews. If the intention is sustained growth of em-

---

* Peter M. Senge, *The Fifth Discipline: The Art & Practice of the Learning Organization* (New York: Doubleday, 2006).

ployees, I think most of us can agree that the traditional review process has the opposite effect.

Working from the premise that learning is key to survival, what role then do leaders play in building a learning organization? An obvious choice might be leaders are teachers. Yes, of course they are. Leaders are coaches. Again, yes, that will certainly be needed from time to time. However, I would say the most important thing a leader can do for his or her survival and that of the company is to stay in "learner" mode. The leader sets an example for everyone around them as a student: how to be curious, inquisitive, open to new ideas, willing to try things, question longstanding assumptions, and see mistakes as an opportunity to learn, rather than an opportunity to blame someone for a failure. The blame game can shut down the learning organization faster than any managerial construct I know. In fact, the blame game creates a different kind of learning construct for team members: how to deflect accountability and never try anything even remotely risky.

If we want to establish a joyful leadership culture where learning is modeled and expected, what kind of "learner" behaviors would we expect to see from our leaders and consequently expect from those we wish to grow into leaders?

Learners Are Readers

There are many approaches to this organizational enlightenment. I believe establishing a strong reading practice within your team will excite the imagination of learners. This activity alone can foster the development of leaders. At Menlo, there are so many books that have contributed to the systems and processes we now employ. As James often says, we didn't invent anything at Menlo; rather we stole every idea (legally) from a book.

A set of recommended books is included at the end of this book. Please, though, do not be satisfied with our book recommendations. Ask leaders you admire what books they are reading or which ones have greatly influenced them. You will be hard pressed to find a great leader who isn't also a reader. (Some leaders prefer listening to audiobooks. That is reading too!)

If you'd like to establish book reading as part of your corporate culture, I'd suggest the following:

Make books widely available. Encourage team members to order books for the company. Establish an unlocked library and don't fret if books go missing. If a favorite book is never available, order another copy.

Consider starting book clubs or a series of Lunch and Learns. Asking someone to read a book and then share what they've learned with others is a great way to cement the lessons and promote presentation skills, which are always valuable. Andrew M. on our team is always reading and regularly shares what he learns with everyone either via our community email thread or Lunch and Learns. I've learned to point Andrew to books I've been meaning to read.

Encourage, reward, promote, support, and/or reimburse people taking classes at local community colleges or local seminars and workshops. These classes will often use helpful books as part of their curriculum. Ask team members who took the class to present what they learned to others on the team.

Create an internal email group or other community messaging system to share interesting articles, TED talks, and the like with the whole team. Encourage active discussions on the material. Three of our senior leaders, Carol M., Lauren H., and Michelle P., are great at finding meaningful TEDx talks and passing them along to our team, including commentary of the lessons they learned.

Consider implementing learning passports (a simple booklet that tracks progress) with explicit goals for reading, taking classes, and so on. In some cases, this may be a component to raises or promotions. I believe this works best when the tracking is done on the honor system and, if there is a reward, it isn't huge. The actual reward should be in the learning, not in the compensation for learning. Zingerman's uses this system for their staff.

Use reading as a jumping-off point to engage more deeply with other leaders and thinkers. If you happen to live near a university as we do in Ann Arbor, ask professors to come in and present their body of work to your team. Most of these professors are published authors. You can honor the professor by making sure you've bought his or her books for the students to dive deeper before or after the presentation. Keep track of new books coming out from those same professors, as they might appreciate a chance to practice a new presentation on willing listeners. This works even better if you can return the favor and allow their students to study your company for their class projects.

You can also encourage your team to attend and present at professional conferences. Encourage your team members to study presenters' work, so they can ask more informed questions. I can tell you from personal experience, authors are delighted to interact on deeper topics with interested audience members.

Learners Seek Role Models

I do a lot of public speaking. I enjoy it, and based on the feedback I receive, I must be pretty good at it by now. For many, though, public speaking ranks just above death as the least favorite activity for people.

Many have asked me for advice on becoming a good public speaker. Thousands of hours of practice certainly help. I think, however, that it is just as important to become a student of great public speakers. Watch those you really admire, in person or online, and ask yourself what it is they do to entrance you with their speaking ability. Watch how they move, how they use humor appropriately, how they use pauses to great effect, how they change their tone throughout the course of their presentation, and how they use the arc of their stories to make a point. Note how prepared they are when they step on the stage and if they use slides, how those visual artifacts support their speaking rather than become the focal point. Pay attention to how they open their talks and how they close them.

Now, this is just for one particular skill, public speaking, but you can find role models for any behavior or ability you want to pick up. The approach is the same: identify leaders and teachers you admire and catalog what you appreciate about them. Consider which of those admirable qualities you can mimic or adopt. The goal is not simply copying and imitation but rather finding the essence of what they do well and how you might incorporate this into your own authentic style.

You might not have to go far to find good teachers and role models. My first public speaking teacher was my dad. He would often have me watch speakers on television and comment to me about their style. Each time I found myself at a conference, or even in church, I would look for examples of good public speaking and then try to figure out why I liked them so much. I would make mental notes of things to try the next time I had the opportunity. I occasionally adapt one of their best stories to fit my talk.

My very first boss at the Macomb Intermediate School District, Bill Banach, is still one of my favorite public speakers. He taught me how to use appropriate humor to keep an audience engaged and how dramatic pauses could really bring a point home. I learned the art of speaking is as much about content as it is delivery and style. Perhaps, most important, he taught me the power of speaking to move minds and make change in the world. I also appreciate that he created opportunities for me to speak. My job was to embrace the opportunities when he offered them to me. He would then offer feedback and lessons. I still have a copy of basic guidelines for great public speaking that he gave me when I was just eighteen years old.

Interface Systems CEO Bob Nero was also an awesome speaker. I seldom saw Bob speaking to groups out in the world, but I did admire how he led Interface through tough times with a calming style when he held all-company meetings. I felt I was being taught the duties of CEO as I watched Bob speak. At the time I didn't know if I would ever be a CEO, but the leadership lessons were invaluable.

Even my cofounder James is one of my heroes in this regard. James's style can be provocative at times, and he swears more than I am comfortable with, but he can get away with it. He never lets you settle into a complacent pattern of thinking about anything. He will present a lesson that feels conventional and then draw the opposite conclusion from what you were expecting. With these mental gymnastics, he stretches your mind. Most of us can follow him when he does this. At times, the effect is so profound we lose him. I've learned simply to stop him there, backtrack, and make sure I don't miss the important point. I've paid a lot of attention to his style and have adopted his best teaching for myself.

If a role model is someone you don't know, the opportunity exists to respectfully build a relationship with them. Reach out, ask them for advice, meet them over coffee if possible, and find out if there are ways you can help them. I have done this with several wonderful professors at the University of Michigan whom I have since gotten to know well. You'd be surprised how easy it is to build a relationship in this way. Obviously, being respectful of their time is key as well. Be sure to nurture these relationships and care about your role model as a person.

Now I often find myself on the mentoring side of the relationship. The best example I have of this in my life is a young man named Terrell. I first met him while visiting the Detroit high school he attended. As a freshman, he was pursuing both programming and entrepreneurship and, when he learned of my visit, he made sure to very respectfully and enthusiastically introduce himself. I was taken with his energy and gave him my card and a few weeks later dropped by to hand deliver a copy of my book, which thrilled him to no end. One day, I received an email from him with the simplest message: "How was your day?"

The first time it happened I just smiled inside at the thoughtfulness. I couldn't help but answer him completely by telling him as much as I could about what my workday was like. This pattern has continued throughout his entire four years of high school. He has also asked me deep questions about life, career, business, entrepreneurship, college, technology, etc. If he hasn't reached out to me in a while, he will apologize for his long absence and then ask me again how things are going. Eventually, I started to write him and ask him how his day was going. This has been a delightful mentor-mentee relationship. He sent me a beautiful handwritten thank-you note filled with gratitude for the time and advice I've given him over the years. Joy.

The Best Leaders Are Learners *and* Teachers

Ari Weinzweig, CEO and cofounder at Zingerman's, is an example of an excellent leader, learner, and teacher. Zingerman's is a role model of an organization that creates great leaders as well. As teachers, Ari and his cofounder, Paul Saginaw, lead the "Welcome to Zingerman's" seminar for every one of their new staff members. That is a big commitment but so important to their work. They choose not to delegate it to someone else.

Bob Chapman, CEO at Barry-Wehmiller, is also a teaching leader. The effect his teaching is having on the culture of his company and the world through his book *Everybody Matters* and his talks, and on students who travel to the Barry-Wehmiller University in Phillips, Wisconsin, is profound. In their own words:

"Originally designed for Barry-Wehmiller associates only, BWU's classes have proven to be so transformational for our team members that in 2011 we began offering our flagship course, Communications Skills Training, to people outside the organization. Since then, we have taught the course to leaders within health care, our military, private and public enterprise as well as nonprofits. By sharing what we've learned with like-minded organizations and individuals, we bring to life Barry-Wehmiller University's vision of using the power of business to build a better world."

I've noticed that the cultures (and the leaders who created them) I most admire have some formal teaching arm as part of their organization. They not only teach themselves, but typically share their lessons with the world. ZingTrain at Zingerman's, Barry-Wehmiller University, Charlie Kim and Meghan Messenger at Next Jump, Richard Branson at Virgin, and the list goes on and on.

Ask yourself whether you can codify any of the insights you've gathered in your company and share them with others. Perhaps your team can host a Lunch and Learn for other companies in your area to share best practices on marketing or team building, for example. We often invite friends and colleagues at other companies into our Lunch and Learns.

We also share our basement space with TechArb, the University of Michigan's student start-up accelerator for Michigan students pursuing their own companies. We regularly invite these student entrepreneurs into Menlo to be taught and mentored by our team. Other entrepreneurial organizations on campus have reached out to us for similar mentoring sessions. Our team will often sit with the students through lunch, giving them feedback on their plans, their ideas, and their approach.

Our team members write blog posts around topics of interest to our industry. They regularly present at local and national conferences. They will also volunteer to visit local schools on career days. We also frequently open our doors for pro-bono tours for elementary, middle, and high school classes. Our team enjoys prepping for these visits because they know they will need a slightly different teaching approach to keep the kids interested during the visit.

Our team formally teaches our processes to others who come from all over the world to learn about our unique approach. We don't have a separate teaching corps. The teachers are the team members who do the day-to-day work for our clients. For some, becoming a teacher is an uncomfortable first foray into public speaking. Yet they find, because they are teaching very interested students a subject they are passionate about, their nerves quickly disappear.

This formality of preparing our courses ends up feeding the student side of our team members and leaders. By teaching others, we are learning. This is especially true as our classes leave a lot of room for Q&A. Since we never know what the questions will be, we end up having to be on our toes to answer questions all day long. Some of our classes last multiple days. Most of our student-teachers are completely exhausted the first few times they teach a new class because their brains and their hearts are so active throughout the entire day. We have learned to always pair teachers so that each pair-teacher can support the other. This stereoscopic teaching method also allows us to grow new teachers, which is, probably unsurprisingly, our first step to growing new leaders.

There is excitement in creating a new class and teaching it for the first time. There is also tremendous learning in what could have made the class better. We fold these improvements into the course materials each time the class is taught.

Our team doesn't wait very long to ask newer team members to start to teach. They will typically start by co-leading tours (with a good pair partner of course). Within weeks of joining Menlo, new team members are co-leading tours. It won't be too long after that when they find themselves co-teaching a class that might be one, two, or three days long.

In addition to learning, our team also loves to scout for new classes to take in and around our community. They have taken classes on programming, project management, design, finance, visioning, and many other subjects. If we read an impactful book and it has classes associated with it, we will often send at least a pair of our team to take the class. We have done this with the lessons from The Arbinger Institute, VitalSmarts, and Zingerman's. We were so taken with the lessons offered in the *Influencer* class from VitalSmarts, we ended up bringing in a train-the-trainer instructor and taught eighteen of our team members how to teach *Influencer* to others.

Pairing: Let Your People Teach Each Other

Of all the systems we have at Menlo, the one that has the greatest impact both on developing teachers and leaders is our paired work model.

Almost everyone at Menlo works in pairs now. When we started the company, only our programmers paired. A couple of years later, we added pairing to our high-tech anthropology practice, as we learned its power and effectiveness from our programmers. Then QA started pairing. We now also loosely pair our project managers, and our front- and back-office staff. We pair when we teach, we often pair when we are in sales conversations, and we pair when we develop class materials.

Our life experience with teaching and learning was strongly modeled for at least thirteen years in the classroom and then some if you went to college. The teacher is in the front, and the students are in the seats. The teacher teaches, the students study. The teacher tests the students and determines how well they learned. A state board of education adds a layer of hierarchy on top of this model with standardized tests, which further demonstrates that the teacher needs a boss too. It is little wonder we build our business organizations the way we do. What alternative models do we have? What if the students were also the teachers? I imagine this is what one-room schoolhouses were like. The fifth graders sat alongside the first graders and helped teach. They likely enjoyed quickly employing their newfound knowledge. Of course, the younger students ask annoying questions that cause the teachers to scratch their head and learn even more. And every once in a while, a precocious youngster would offer up a kernel of unexpected wisdom that caused new learning by the older students. This is exactly what we have in Menlo's one-room schoolhouse for innovation. Each week we pair our team members, one with another. The teaching and learning is going in both directions all day long.

And . . . in our big open room, with nearly everyone paired and in constant conversation all day long, you hear the sounds of teaching, and you can sense the development of budding leaders as they solve problems together. In this problem-solving mode, if one pair partner has an idea, they must lead the other person to their idea, explaining, thinking out loud, answering questions, and leaving themselves open to the idea that their idea is incorrect, incomplete, or needs improvement. You can imagine the cascade of leadership development that occurs when you get to practice teaching and are being taught almost every minute of every day. Further, the pairs switch often, at least once a week. The approach for leading one person may differ from another, so you will learn in our environment how to teach, learn, and lead with different styles.

There are many opportunities as well to learn and teach in a larger group setting. Because we work shoulder to shoulder with no walls, and the project teams have all their tables pushed together, there is always the serendipity of hearing the ideas of another pair and chiming in on the discussion that is occurring just a few feet away. This might lead to a quick jump up to a whiteboard and an impromptu brainstorming session to solve a problem that requires six heads rather than just two.

Our weekly kickoffs for each project team are another chance to practice teaching and leading others. In these sessions, the entire project team is gathered together, away from their computers, walking through the *team* plan for the entire week. In this way, each pair gets to hear what all the other pairs are working on in their group and reflects on the best strategies for the overall work, not just their own piece. Many lively discussions ensue during these sessions.

Our weekly Show and Tells bring us together with our customers. We must teach and be taught by someone who is paying us for our work. The style of our customers varies wildly from company to company. Our methods and approaches may not match theirs (it typically does not), so we must learn to lead in different ways with various methods of influence within the course of projects that can last months or years.

Never Let a Good Mistake Go to Waste

Lisa joined us in 2007 right after she graduated from the University of Illinois. During her laborious job search after college, a friend suggested to her that she look at the list of "Best and Brightest" companies to work for in the Midwest, and she stumbled upon Menlo. She did some research and felt this could be the place. She traveled to Ann Arbor and went through our Extreme Interview. She made it through the interview process and joined the team as a Project Manager.

Shortly into her tenure, she took over the PM role for the

Accuri project, our biggest and most complex project to date. Fortunately, in our world, the PMs aren't left to fend for themselves, as they are surrounded and supported by their peers on the projects.

One of our customary practices is to ship to our client an installable CD/DVD every week with the software we've completed to date, so they can play with the software on their own while we continue working. Lisa made sure we did this every week for our customer.

One week the "completed software" didn't work. Rare for us, but not that unusual for a project as complex as this. This version wouldn't be shipping to Accuri customers, so it wasn't that big of a setback or problem, as the problems would be corrected in the next cycle. However, Lisa decided we would still go through the motions of our standard process and build and ship the DVD to Accuri even though the software wouldn't run. It was our standard process, after all, and a practice our customer had come to expect. Lisa included a note with the DVD indicating that while the software didn't work, we still wanted to follow our process and send along an installable but broken piece of software.

Our customer was not happy. It wasn't the broken software that upset them. It was the fact that our team seemed to be blindly following a process that provided zero value to the customer and cost project dollars that could have been better spent either fixing the problem or adding another feature.

Lisa didn't get the angry email from our client, but my cofounder James did. His next move was key to growing a future leader.

James calmly went over to Lisa and walked through the lesson of making sure we are always thinking about client value when applying our standard process. He further explained it is OK to make on-the-fly decisions and deviate if the situation warrants it. She should always be comfortable saying, "I'm not sure what to do" in any given circumstance and ask for guidance. In this way, she can develop a stronger internal compass for decision making.

James's lesson was delivered over eight years ago. Lisa is one of our senior leaders now and still tells the story like it was yesterday. She became a better project manager that day, and she found that through encouragement confidence builds and personal growth can happen. This lesson gave her important insights on what it means to patiently develop leaders.

Lisa saw a similar scenario play out for another team member. She was able to recall this old leadership lesson and remind us of its importance. In this way, the student became the teacher. As it turned out, her student was me. I was away on a European speaking trip and I saw, via email, a mistake being made (in my opinion) by another team member. With only the benefit of email, I intervened—not as a teacher but as boss. So rather than use the mistake as an opportunity to teach, I just made sure the team member knew I didn't like what was happening and, of course, expected it to be fixed. (Not much joyful leadership here, eh?) I returned to the office a few days later and Lisa was upset and let me know. We talked about it and got a chance to air both sides in person. A few days later, she pulled me aside and had crafted a thoughtful mind map to show me what our strongest values were and what I could have done differently in that situation. She even used some stories from our history (including the one I wrote above about her and

James) to draw lessons and describe the hope she had for the future. Fortunately, I grew a lot that day with Lisa as my teacher.

If you want to create great leaders, you must keep those leaders
in learning mode. They must stay curious and hungry students.
Then they must learn to pass those lessons along to others on the
team. To keep this cycle going, your leaders need to develop one
more important skill to keep the learning vibrant and alive—telling
stories.

CHAPTER 13

Become Storytellers

Tell me the facts and I'll learn. Tell me the truth and I'll believe. But tell me a story and it will live in my heart forever.

—**Native American proverb**

I WAS BLESSED TO HAVE A DAD WHO WAS AND REMAINS A HERO TO me. He passed away in 2008, just shy of his ninetieth birthday. He loved spending time with his three boys and was always so proud of us. The love both my mom and dad surrounded us with as children has profoundly and positively impacted me in ways I still find remarkable.

My dad loved the outdoors. This love, developed from camping trips in northern Michigan with his own father back in the 1920s, is what led him to be the Scoutmaster of Boy Scout Troop 145, where my two older brothers earned the rank of Life Scout, and me, Eagle Scout. His favorite kind of camping trip involved canoeing. He even bought a green canvas wood-ribbed canoe so we could go canoeing whenever we wanted.

In the summer of 1968, Dad asked me if I'd like to take a week-long trip down the Manistee River, a beautifully quiet river in Northern Michigan. We would start in Grayling, bring all our camping gear with us, and spend a week traveling west down this glorious river. The trip would end in Mesick, Michigan, well along the way to the outlet of the river into Lake Michigan. I couldn't be more excited to spend an entire week with my dad on such a grand adventure paddling across half our state into what I thought would be a pure wilderness adventure.

The wilderness wasn't exactly as I had imagined—the river passed under many roads and bridges and most nights we spent at official campgrounds that nestled themselves up against the Manistee. Even so, the days were filled with quiet times along this meandering, gentle river through vast state forests. Blue jays called out their warnings to their friends ahead as we slipped down the glimmering waterway. Some days, it gently rained on us during the trip and we passed the time, paddling with our army-surplus ponchos on, singing "Wait 'Till the Sun Shines, Nellie."

One late afternoon, needing a brief break, we pulled up to a sandy shoreline spot and noticed a warning sign that told us to keep out. We decided to just take a quick break and be on our way. As we were almost to shore, the canoe hit a sharp rock in the shallow riverbed, poking a dime-sized hole in the green canvas. The canoe took on water quickly. We were miles from a town and we likely couldn't canoe our way to a repair option with this hole in the bottom of the canoe and keep our packs of food, clothing, and camping gear dry.

As we left the canoe and climbed up the riverbank into the forbidden company land, my heart skipped a beat. This was exactly the kind of campsite I was hoping for the entire trip—a very secluded rustic site with a clearing and no one else within miles. The joy of my ten-year-old adventurer emerged, and I asked Dad if we could spend the night here. He didn't hesitate. We set up camp and starting cooking dinner.

After dinner, he grabbed the leftover tin from our dinner of tuna fish and told me to go search out some pine tar chips from the many pines surrounding our little forest retreat. I scraped them into the tin, not quite sure what he was up to. He put the tin over our fire and told me to go find some birch bark.

I came back with some palm-size pieces of birch bark. We headed down to the canoe with the tin of melted pine tar and birch bark. We turned the canoe upside down, and he proceeded to pour the liquid pine tar around the hole in the bottom. He then asked me to take a piece of the birch bark and carefully press it into the pine tar and hold it until the tar cooled and congealed.

I was stunned.

He explained that he had recently read a book on how the Native Americans crafted their birch bark canoes and applied those lessons to fix our canoe. I can't fully convey, in words, the depth of magic this moment had for me. We were in the wilderness and using the skills of Native Americans from hundreds of years ago. This is the stuff of pure adventure and imagination for a ten-year-old.

After we returned home, my dad got the biggest kick out of my storytelling to all my friends as I gathered them around the canoe in the backyard and regaled them with stories of high adventure in the wilderness and the life-saving lessons I learned from my dad. He told me years later that he was almost always nearby doing yard work and listening, with delight, to my storytelling.

Two Arts Are Intertwined: Leading and Storytelling

That summer of 1968 taught me the intoxicating lesson of the power of storytelling. I can recall, in my younger days, thinking I would never be as good a storyteller as my dad. To be honest, I didn't think I would ever have stories like he did, and I didn't think I would ever remember enough details to tell them. I certainly didn't know how to tell them well.

Storytelling plays a significant role in creating an intentional culture. As leaders we are responsible for curating the stories we want shared and teaching others on our team the art of capturing and telling stories. There are many things a leader must do (and not do), but among the most important is storytelling, a leadership tradition as old as human civilization. Stories connect us from heart to mind, from spirit to body, from concept to reality.

If culture eats strategy for breakfast, then storytelling sets the table for the meal. In essence, we tell stories so we can pass the art, responsibility, and great joy of leadership down to others and share what we know with those in our community.

Storytelling enters our daily work in many different ways. The most obvious way we tell our stories is by sharing them with the myriad tours we give and in the many classes we teach. We found our lessons are conveyed so much more effectively and remembered so much better through storytelling than any other means.

We use storytelling during our sales conversations to help others understand why we work the way we do. We tell stories of past project successes, and we capture stories of failure so that those unfamiliar with the challenges of our kind of work can better understand why we do what we do.

Finally, we tell stories to each other. This might occur during the workday, especially with newer staff, so that they understand the intent of our approach and feel connected to our history, beyond the few months or years they've been with us. We will also tell stories after hours in the bar for a good laugh. If we end up in a long car ride together going to see a client, we'll spend the ride telling stories. I have also found that team members who travel with me to distant cities for conferences or client visits enjoy the chance for an evening of CEO storytelling at dinner (at least that's what they tell me).

Many of the stories we tell each other involve great difficulties from our past that led to important decisions about why the company operates the way it does. You can imagine if you get to the place where emergencies aren't commonplace, you have to rely on stories to remind people of why we do what we do or else it will seem superfluous and almost unnecessary to be so rigorous and disciplined about our approach.

For example, the last time our team recalls a true software emergency was in 2004 when we were rebuilding the Organ Transplant Information System. A kidney had become available for a patient, but the patient record could not be retrieved. It was on a Saturday and we were all home enjoying time with our families. The hospital needed our help and time was of the essence. A life was at stake. They were able to contact one of our team members at home, the record was retrieved, and the operation proceeded successfully. We can use this story with our newer team members so that they are aware of how important all our practices are because software often holds the lives of people.

Another famous sales story was about a project that we didn't get. In our early days, we tried a traditional sales approach and our sales guy brought us a deal that he wanted our help in closing. James and I speculated it would need to be priced at least $200,000. Our sales guy said the customer only had $60,000, and if we wanted to win the deal, we'd have to price it at $60,000. We told him to pass. He got very upset with us and demanded we drop our price to $60,000. We refused, and we lost the deal to another company in town. A few years later the CEO of that company came to visit me and wondered if we'd like to take over the software development part of their business, as they weren't having much luck in that area because it wasn't core to their overall business. He went on to tell me about a bad deal they closed a couple of years ago for $60,000, and then ended up spending over $200,000 to finish it. If they kept closing deals like that, they'd go out of business. I just smiled. This story, told again and again within our walls, reinforces why we might say no to a client project even when we need the work. There are no shortcuts in our world, just old-fashioned hard work that takes time and money and no amount of wishing it were different can change this hard truth.

Many of the stories I am asked to tell are like the arc of the story in this book and *Joy, Inc.* How did we think of building Menlo the way we did? What had we tried along the way, and why did we settle on the model we did?

Stories Are Infectious, Especially When Your Customers Are Drawn into Them

The most satisfying aspect of our storytelling culture is when we draw our customers into the stories and *they* want to retell them when they are with us. A storytelling culture is clearly infectious. I remember one visit with a customer named Don, who was a very high-level executive from an automotive supplier. We ran several surprising and memorable experiments with Don and his team while they were visiting us. The next time we saw him at his offices in Tennessee, he spent several minutes telling his colleagues the story of his unique and remarkable visit to Menlo.

It is likely Don and his team are going to be Menlo customers for a long time. This is the beauty of storytelling. It creates very human ties that are not easily broken. I like that personally and professionally.

To tell stories, you have to curate them. The future we hope for can be found in the stories we tell over and over.

What I have noticed in the last few years at Menlo is that we are now lucid story *curators*. I borrow this term from the idea of lucid dreaming, in which the dreamer is aware that he or she is dreaming and can use this awareness to modestly direct the dream itself. Because we are now such active storytellers, we see stories as they are unfolding and have an intrinsic sense that "this" is going to be an important story to tell over and over again. In this way, we are capturing the story details quicker rather than days, months, or years later. We can also capture more of the richness of the context so that we know better why this story is so important. As the story unfolds, we now will find ourselves asking deeper questions about details that led to the moment we are seeing. We might ask how it came about, what part of our culture or values led to the moment we are witnessing. In this way, our stories become richer and more meaningful for us, and for those who ask us questions about our stories. The net effect is that our storytelling can go very deep if the listener is intrigued enough to ask lots of questions. My daughter Megan once commented to me, during a class I was teaching, that she was amazed how deep our lessons went. She said, "Dad, when I was in college, the professor might be able to go down one or two levels of questions on any given topic, but there doesn't seem to be any end to the depth you can go when you tell Menlo stories."

Stories Flow in All Directions

One of our longtime team members once told me that every time a tour went by where he was working, he would stop working for a minute and listen to what we were saying. He remarked that even though they were the same stories over and over, he never tired of them. He also expressed his amazement at how I could tell these old stories in a way that made it seem like I was telling them for the first time.

Up until this feedback, though, I had not considered the effect of the stories on the Menlonians who heard them each time I led a tour. It makes complete sense to me now. These were stories of our greatest triumphs, our history, our hopes, our aspirations, our dreams, and our mission and how we brought it to life in our work. Why wouldn't team members, not just tour members, want to hear and be inspired by these stories?

It was about this time the team playfully started calling me Chief Storyteller. Once I realized how valuable this role was to inspiring our team and deeply instilling the values of our intentional culture into their hearts, I added this playful title to my business card.

The storytelling on the tours also drew team members into the mix, as our guests wouldn't just want to hear stories from the CEO. If someone asked a question that I felt a team member had more practical insight into, I would ask that team member or pair to answer their question. Our guests love those direct interactions with our team.

I also had a regular sequence I would do with the team, where I would explain the colorful status dots on the story cards of our work authorization boards. Each column of cards under a pair's name would outline that pair's work for the week. I would explain that a yellow sticky dot on a card in their lane implies that is the work they are doing right now. As each card had a unique number on it, I would verify the system by calling out to the pair:

"Hey Rob, hey Chris—what card are you working on right now?"

They would answer with the number of the card they were working on, and our guests would see the alignment immediately between our visual artifacts and the actual work being done. Except when it didn't. Then the team would offer up some reason as to why the dot wasn't up-to-date. This started to happen more often.

One day, as a tour group was forming in the front of our space, as I turned to guide them in and start telling our stories, I saw a bunch of our team members jump out of their chairs, walk up to the work authorization boards, and start updating the sticky dots.

Boom! The tours, the storytelling, and the predictable pattern of my callouts rejuvenated the team's accountability to a process we believed in but had started to get a little lax about. As the years went by, our visual artifacts became increasingly accurate, because the team believed in the stories I was telling, and they wanted them to be true. This is part of the power of a strong storytelling culture. You repeat the stories of the things you most believe about your-selves. And the things you most *want* to believe about yourselves.

I also began to realize how much the stories were also holding me accountable. If team members were hearing my stories on nearly every tour, they could hold me accountable to the content and the intent of the stories. I would never have wanted a team member to approach me after a tour and say "Hey Rich, that company you were describing on the tour sounds amazing. Where are they located?"

Crafting a Team of Storytellers

As our tour counts and frequency increased, we started averaging almost one tour every business day of the year. As you might imagine, the workload of the Chief Storyteller was increasing to an unsustainable level. James would also lead tours, but I still did a lot of them. I enjoyed them, but as CEO, author, and public speaker, I did have a lot of other things to do. My days started getting longer and longer.

The team realized it wasn't sustainable and that in many ways my role had become the kind of tower of knowledge we were trying to avoid in other areas of the business. I was back to hero mode (old habits die hard). They suggested that I start to share the duties of leading tours. Of course, we then fell back on the central lesson of the company, and they started pairing me with another Menlonian on the tour. I had to learn to quiet my voice and allow space for my pair partner to lead the tour. This was hard for me, but I got better at it.

During these paired tours, I heard two kinds of stories. First,

I heard my own stories, retold through the lens of a team member. They weren't told exactly as I would tell them, but I resisted the temptation to correct the retelling, especially if the fact changes weren't material to the point of the story.

More important, I began to hear *other people's* stories. These were stories I had never heard before, and they were fascinating. To me. I was now getting a deeper insight to the company I had cofounded. I became the student as I witnessed the birth of new storytellers.

I also learned that my stories weren't always perfectly accurate. One story I told repeatedly over the years was about a project we did for the local county government. Michelle, who became one of my pair partners on the tour, reminded me after one tour that she was one of the characters in the story and that the story I told wasn't *exactly* the way it went. I asked her for the real story so I could retell it more accurately. She said, "Oh no, I love the way you tell the story and the changes wouldn't affect the point you are making."

In this moment, I realized there is another fundamental truth about stories. The exact facts aren't anywhere near as important as how the stories themselves make you feel.

The Sum of Mission, Values, Culture, and Storytelling

The art of storytelling is as old as human history. Before books or schools, leaders would use an oral tradition to pass on the most important lessons of their families, their tribes, and their nations around campfires, at the foot of totems, or by singing anthems that had captured these tales of their history. Mankind has preserved and fostered the growth of civilization through story. Storytelling touches our hearts and minds in ways that policy manuals and fancy brochures never will. As leaders trying to foster a culture of joyful leadership, we cannot ignore this time-honored tradition. Our mission, our vision, and our values must be ever present in these stories. We should also capture the stories of the mistakes we made and tell those stories too.

Storytelling itself is a skill that needs to be developed, honored, and nurtured. If you do not already have a storytelling culture, set out to build one. Find avenues to tell stories. For us, this started with tours of our company. For you, you may use stories in new employee orientation to tell the history of the company to those just joining. If you like, set up your own internal TEDxOurCompany event and ask the presenters to bring stories of work to the event. Record them. Run the event every year.

With our mission to "end human suffering in the world as it relates to technology," we have captured many stories where there was suffering and we were able to end it. We tell those stories again and again, to the world and ourselves. Visitors come from all over the world to hear our stories told and retold. We have many repeat visitors. Some of our best customers have come to us through these visits. Some visitors go out and tell our stories to others, who then come to visit. They want to see if the stories are true. The fact that our entire team is called to be storytellers creates an even more powerful effect on each other and the world.

Of the myriad practices we have in place, there is no question that storytelling plays a big role in both fostering our culture and fostering the growth of our leaders. A team, who has chosen to work for a company like ours, wants to believe there is alignment among the leaders. If the stories that leaders tell with great passion produce a feeling of alignment within the team itself, they will feel safe and comforted instead of disconnected and on edge about what is expected. They will know what our most important stories are, and they will want to be part of them. They will continue to share stories and build new ones across all kind of teams, companies, communities, even nations.

Bigger Than Ourselves

The final test of a leader is that he or she leaves behind in others the conviction and the will to carry on.

—Walter Lippmann

I WAS SIX YEARS OLD THE FIRST TIME I SAW MY FATHER CRY. IT would be rare to witness that again in my lifetime. I can see him in his armchair, in the living room (right near the place where a few years later I would situate that bookshelf), sitting silently with tears rolling down his face. The Kennedy funeral march was proceeding through Washington on the television on that late November day in 1963. Just a few days earlier I had heard the announcement at school over the PA system in my first-grade classroom that the president had been shot.

Kennedy exemplifies for me the type of inspirational leader who knew how to carry the day and a nation with oration. I have always admired the power of the written and spoken word. Kennedy's words inspire me to this day. He shared so many memorable, inspirational calls to grand purpose in his speeches. One called us to the Peace Corps, another to the moon *and back,* but one that I will always remember is his grandest call to service:

"Ask not what your country can do for you—ask what you can do for your country."

Those words inspired a nation to consider others before themselves. I have carried these lessons in my heart since those tearful moments in the living room watching my dad grieve over the funeral procession of the flag-draped coffin of his fallen hero.

It's Not about Us; It's about Other People

As you consider your next steps on a joyful leadership journey and how you can both be inspired and be an inspiration to others, ask yourself whom you serve and what great and joyful service looks like for them.

We at Menlo speak often of our desire to "end human suffering in the world as it relates to technology." This is first and foremost an external focus on those we serve. The people who pay for software to be designed and built often suffer a loss of patience and willpower as projects spin out of control with no logical end in sight. We think about the people who end up using the software every day, who our industry came to call "stupid users." They suffer because no one ever thought of them when the software was being designed and built.

In your business, you can always identify an opportunity to be of service to others. You may have your own version of human suffering that you are trying to end, and in doing so, bringing joy to the world and to those you serve, and ultimately joy to yourself knowing that you made a small improvement in the world around you.

Much of what I have learned and applied over the years is based on what I have come to recognize as basic needs that feed human energy. I have come to believe there are some basic needs of human nature that can fill our hearts with inspired purpose:

We want to work on something *much* bigger than ourselves.

We can only do that if we work in community with one another.

We are energized by a lofty external goal in service to others.

This outward mind-set brings out the best version of us. If we, as leaders, can inspire those around us with a clear vision of serving others, working with pride, and delivering outstanding results to the world, most other things become far less important. We will hear less about *"my* office," *"my* title," and *"my* stuff." It's amazing what we will put up with and fight through when we have a worthy mission in front of us. This mind-set will inspire those around you to their own leadership journey.

Leave the Campsite Better Than You Found It

A few years ago, I spent an hour on a webcast with venture capitalist and marketing guru Guy Kawasaki and Huffington Post founder

Arianna Huffington, discussing wellness and productivity. The conversations wrapped up with a simple question: "Rich, how do you want to be remembered?"

I recall from my Boy Scout days the idea that when you planted your tent at a campsite and later pulled up stakes to move on, you wanted to "leave the campsite better than you found it."

I think the campsite we all call planet Earth is the place I want to feel I left better than I found it. Whether that is how people remember me is less important to me than knowing in my own heart that my contributions left our shared campsite a little better than I found it. To the extent I can do this every single day as a leader at work—and can help others do this too—I find my calling and my fulfillment.

I wish you great success in your own quest for joyful leadership and the impact it can create in the lives of others.

The Positive Organization

The greatest competitive advantage in our modern economy is a positive and engaged brain.

—Shawn Achor

IN THE EARLIEST YEARS OF MENLO, I ATTENDED A PRESENTATION by Dr. Bob Quinn, a professor at the University of Michigan Ross School of Business. Bob was giving a presentation on *empowerment* with a delivery that, for me, finally brought that tired business term to life.

At some point during the talk, I realized that there were probably very few other leaders in the room who had truly experienced the kind of radical empowerment Bob was talking about. I approached Bob after the talk and asked him if he realized that no one in the room understood what he was describing. He said, "I know that, Rich, but my question is . . . why do *you* know that?" I couldn't explain my feelings to Bob as much as I could show him my understanding by introducing him to our culture and our beliefs. I could tell in hearing this talk that Bob and I believed the same things about how to lead others. Bob was telling us that empowerment wasn't something you could *do* for someone else, but as a leader, you could set the conditions and cultural setting that would make empowerment occur spontaneously and naturally. In effect, Bob was saying that empowerment is such a natural place for human beings to end up that we actually have to take explicit actions to ensure its demise. And these leadership actions of fear-based motivation, micromanaging control, and continually making sure everyone knows who is the boss are commonplace in modern organizations. If we are lamenting the lack of empowered and engaged employees and want change, we must turn inward and examine our leadership approach.

I invited him to Menlo and showed him the style of empowerment he was describing in action. He smiled broadly and hugged me. In return, he invited me into his world, The Center for Positive Organizations at the Ross Business School. This center conducts research in the way any academic institution does: they study deviant behavior and try to explain how it comes about and what lessons we can take from the behavior to modify our own. What is different about the Center, though, is that rather than study negative deviant behavior and figure out what went wrong and how to fix it, they study positive deviant behavior and how to replicate it.

Every year, the team at the Center hosts the Positive Business

Conference. It's one of the strangest gatherings of businesspeople you will ever witness. It's like finding an oasis in the middle of the business-culture desert; water is flowing in the form of positive ideas for building sustainable business cultures. This crowd believes in people and their potential. For those of us who sometimes feel quite alone in our pursuit of a different kind of organization, these kinds of gatherings can provide inspiration for months.

I believe that positivity is fundamental to not only starting the leadership journey but also keeping it going, especially in difficult times. Consider the wisdom of Ralph Waldo Emerson, who reminded us "you become what you think about all day long." If you fill your head with negative thoughts, surround yourself with pessimistic thinkers, read books, articles, and Facebook posts that confirm your worst instincts about people and leaders, and generally splash around in this swamp, you will become that person. There is another way, the path toward a better way of being. If you approach business—if you approach the hard work of leadership—with positivity, you will reap great rewards.

I'm so grateful for the example and inspiration of positive thinkers, from authors like Tom Peters, Peter Drucker, Shawn Achor, Patrick Lencioni, Frans Johansson, Stan Slap, and Simon Sinek, to the leaders of organizations like Barry-Wehmiller, Zingerman's, VitalSmarts, The Arbinger Institute, WorldBlu, The Center for Positive Organizations at Ross, and The Center for Innovative Cultures at Westminster College. These folks all taught me that business as usual wasn't my only course and that I could reclaim positivity and use it to my advantage.

Stay positive. Know that you can imagine and create a better future for yourself and your organization. Know that the good fight is worth fighting. Know that you have a lot of support and inspiration all around you to take it on, if you just look for it.

I hope you'll stay in touch and share your own leadership journey with me and share the lessons you've learned in thinking about the transformation of the leadership culture in your organization.

You can reach me via @menloprez on Twitter and LinkedIn.

ACKNOWLEDGMENTS

A book is never a solo accomplishment. Yes, it was my (two index) fingers on the keyboard, and that is such an honorable place to sit as a new book comes to life. But know that while it is my name on the cover, I had help—lots of help. I'd like to take some time to recognize some people, some places, and some things that got me this far in the writing process.

To My Family . . .

The families of authors know better than anyone that their loved one disappears during the writing and editing process. The same is true for speakers who travel, and just as much for CEOs of companies they found. You, my wonderful family, have enjoyed all three over the last eighteen months. I could not have done this without your love and encouragement. I am grateful every time you are near me. I thank you for all the pieces of my life you picked up in my absence.

Carol—your love has sustained me in ways I will never be able to describe in words. Your patience, your confidence, and your willingness to live through the fears of being the wife of an entrepreneur make you the rock upon which I have built a life worth living. The fact that you've joined me in this adventure both at home and at work is joy beyond imagination.

Megan, Lauren, Sarah—I would love to take some credit for your strength, your confidence, and your life smarts. However, that credit belongs mostly with your mom. You have taken advantage of every opportunity life has put in front of you. I'm so proud of you all. Megan, your growth as wife, mom, and leader at work is a joy to behold. Lauren, your constant pursuit of adventure in life, work, and school is remarkable and makes me proud. Sarah, your perseverance in the face of daunting health challenges demonstrates a resiliency that is unfathomable to me. Your recovery thus far has me so excited about your future. The love you all have showered me with will carry me for the rest of my days.

Miller—oh, our beautiful little three-year-old granddaughter Mimi. My heart swells each time I am with you. You remind me so fondly of the time raising our own wonderful girls. Your sense of humor is already so obvious. You are pure joy. Your Pop-pop loves you so much! Your mom and dad, Megan and Brian, are doing such a great job raising you. Don't say "No!" so much to them, even when they say "Because I said so!" when you ask why.

Hayden—you've just entered this wonderful world. Your big sister, Mimi, is there to teach you everything she's learned (and it's a lot). She has already given you a nickname that will stick for a long time: Sookie. I can't wait to watch you grow.

My brothers—Mike and Brian, a guy couldn't ask for two better brothers. I don't see you as often as I'd like, but every time we are together, it is as if no time has passed. I'm certain that having two older brothers like the two of you has had more effect on me than I will ever realize. Much of my story is your story too.

Harold and Joan—Mom and Dad, God placed two wonderful in-laws in my life who have been there in so many ways at every turn. Thank you for raising such a wonderful daughter. You perfectly eased the loss of my own parents by being mom and dad to me in every loving way possible. Thank you for your love for me as a son. Mom, we lost you as this book was coming to life. Your influence and love will last forever.

Tina Withers—if I had a fan club, I'd make you president. Your loving support has been such a delight for me. Thanks for spreading the joy in south Florida!

To My Business Partner . . .

James—we've been together for nineteen years now. I still love saying yes to your crazy ideas. And they mostly work out the way we want them to, and when they don't, we work together as trusted friends to make things as good as possible. I couldn't ask for more in a business partner. Thank you for your friendship and for allowing me to win at golf most days.

To Menlonians . . .

To Menlonians—wherever this book may find you. Your willingness to "Run the Experiment" of joining us, even if only for a short time, has made all the difference. I learn so much from all of you. Thank you all for speaking the truth when I need to hear it.

To Anna—my most-often pair partner at work. Your grace,

your steadiness, and your hard work have helped me be the best me I can be. Thank you for always smoothing out all the rough edges of my hectic travel schedule, for helping me find the time to write while juggling all my other CEO priorities, and looking out for all of me, not just the work part of me. You are a blessing.

To Technology . . .

MacBook Air—you were there working under my fingertips every time I needed you. I complain a lot about technology, but never about you.

Scrivener—you are an author's friend. I loved creating my manuscript with you.

Microsoft Word—you served me well during the editing process. Thank you for never letting me down.

Pandora—your playlists kept me focused and productive. Thanks for putting me in the writing mode and mood.

Bose—your noise-canceling properties and comfort gave Pandora the best venue to keep me calm.

Coffee—you are an old "technology," but I couldn't have done this without you. I love you, coffee.

To Places . . . and One Person that Made One Place Special for Me . . .

The Michigan Union—just up the front steps of the Union, past the brass disc in the step memorializing where Kennedy announced the Peace Corps, the first room on the right is as classic a place for writing as any you will find. You were my morning writing place.

Arnetha Harris—If you are reading this, it means you finally got to read the book you so lovingly enquired about and encouraged me about each time I saw your smiling face. You are an inspiration to many others and to me. Your heart, your eyes, your smile, your soul beam love in every direction. Your selfless work of keeping the Michigan Union in tip-top shape made a huge difference to my efforts. You make me so proud to be a Michigan alum because you truly embody what makes Michigan great. Thank you for your friendship and "Go Blue!"

The Michigan Law Library—your Hogwarts style carried me each afternoon I wrote in your lovely setting.

To My Fitness Pals . . .

Jes Reynolds—at fifty, I declared I would be in better shape at sixty than I was at fifty. For five years I proved that simply saying that didn't do anything. Then I found you. Your gentleness (ha!) and encouragement got me to my goal. Now, your next job is to get me in the best shape of my adult life by sixty-four.

Ryan Sullivan—there is so much I could write about you. First and foremost, the love you have showered on my Sarah is such joy for me to see. You two are such a perfect match. Your extra work with me as your client at A2 Functional Fitness is so satisfying every time I finish and I'm still alive.

Mary Mattson—most of what I do physically . . . strengthening and stretching, is in the pursuit of preparing my body for golf. However, if workouts alone were enough for good golf, fitness studios would be filled across the nation. No, every golfer needs a patient, kind, and gentle teacher. That I found you, and graciously shared you with James (ha!), is joy even when my game isn't improving. There are so many leadership lessons in golf, and you are a perfect example of everything that is right with the game. Thank you for your friendship and encouragement.

To Friends . . .

I am so blessed to have so many great friends. I could spend a page on each of you. Please know how much I appreciate you all!

Bob Nero, Jen Baird, Karen Martin, Diana Wong, Kathy Macdonald, Mike Rother, Mark Rosenthal, Jeff Liker, Bo Burlingham, Leigh Buchanan, Tom Peters, Karen Martin, Dalton Li, Ron Sail, Dominique Coster, Suzanne Cislo, Ari Weinzweig, The Center for Positive Organizations, Pastor Dan Flynn, John U. Bacon, Concordia University (thank you for the honorary PhD—I'm Dr. Sheridan now), Westminster College, VitalSmarts, Arbinger Institute, Barry-Wehmiller, Jim and Mary Morgan, The Lean Enterprise Institute, Lean Frontiers, Pétur Arason, Josh Linkner, and so many others!

To My Agent . . .

John Willig—your constant support and advisement has allowed me to check off "write a book" on my bucket list. Twice! Thank you for your work at Literary Services, Inc. You provide such a great haven for authors.

To My Editors . . .

Natalie Horbachevsky—I worked for a year on a manuscript and at that point it felt as though I had simply carved a rough chunk of granite out of a mountainside. Then your work with me started, and in a short two months, you stood behind me and guided me in cutting and shaping that rough piece of rock into a beautiful work of art. It feels like a miracle to have gotten this far in such a short time. Your skill, your guidance, your encouragement, and most of all your focus on the reader is such a perfect example of "Whom do you serve?" that I should have written a chapter just about you. Of course, you would have edited it out. . . . That most readers will get to know me and not you is a shame, because this book is as much your book as it is mine. Thank you for your trust, your friendship, and your partnership.

Linda Irvin—you didn't get involved this time around, but you were there in spirit. I could still hear your voice in my head from our work together on *Joy, Inc.* Thank you for making me a better writer. It made this book easier to write.

To Portfolio at Penguin Random House . . .

Niki Papadopoulos—you and your team at Portfolio placed another bet on me. Thank you. You gave me the space, the time, and the latitude to pursue the joy that is this next book. Then you graciously put Natalie back in my life. I can't thank you enough. I believe that Portfolio is the best place for a business book author to land.

To Mom and Dad . . .

You are gone, but I know you are watching over me from a lovely setting together in heaven. You both would have hit the century mark by now. The love you showered on me and Mike and Brian is evident in so many ways. That love has graced the next two generations. Your three sons had nine loving children whom you adored, and those in turn have had thirteen great-grandchildren (and counting!). You both have created a legacy worthy of a cathedral. Anything that is joyful in my life started with the two of you.

Recommended Teachers

To create a culture of joyful leadership, you must build a learning organization. For us at Menlo Innovations, authors are our teachers and our bookshelves are filled with books that inspire and inform us. I would encourage you to start a library at your company. Then take whatever steps you can to encourage your team to always be in books, reading, learning, sharing, and teaching. There are so many books that have filled our minds with compelling ideas, there is no way to capture all of them here.

My simple advice to you is this: ask people you admire for recommendations, check the books I mention here as well. Read the first few pages of any book and see if the book grabs your attention. If it does, keep reading. If not, set it down for now and find another that does. The relationship between author and reader is a unique one. Only you will know which books are right for you right now.

Here are some of our favorite leadership resources at Menlo:

Books

Getting Things Done: The Art of Stress-Free Productivity by David Allen

Leadership and Self-Deception: Getting Out of the Box by the Arbinger Institute

The Anatomy of Peace: Resolving the Heart of Conflict by the Arbinger Institute

The Outward Mindset: Seeing beyond Ourselves by the Arbinger Institute

It's Your Ship: Management Techniques from the Best Damn Ship in the Navy by Michael Abrashoff

Extreme Programming Explained: Embrace Change by Kent Beck (First Edition)

Small Giants: Companies That Choose to Be Great Instead of Big by Bo Burlingham

Everybody Matters: The Extraordinary Power of Caring for Your People Like Family by Bob Chapman and Raj Sisodia

Creativity at Work: Developing the Right Practices to Make Innovation Happen by Jeff DeGraff and Katherine A. Lawrence

Management: Tasks, Responsibilities, Practices by Peter Drucker

The Systems Bible: The Beginner's Guide to Systems Large and Small by John Gall

The E-Myth Revisited: Why Most Small Businesses Don't Work and What to Do about It by Michael E. Gerber

The Click Moment: Seizing Opportunity in an Unpredictable World by Frans Johansson

The Medici Effect: What Elephants and Epidemics Can Teach Us about Innovation by Frans Johansson

Changing the Way We Change: Gaining Control of Major Operational Change by Jeanenne LaMarsh

The Advantage: Why Organizational Health Trumps Everything Else in Business by Patrick Lencioni

The Five Dysfunctions of a Team: A Leadership Fable by Patrick Lencioni

Getting Naked: A Business Fable about Shedding the Three Fears That Sabotage Client Loyalty by Patrick Lencioni

The Ideal Team Player: How to Recognize and Cultivate the Three Essential Virtues by Patrick Lencioni

The Toyota Way to Service Excellence: Lean Transformation in Service Organizations by Jeffrey K. Liker and Karyn Ross

Turn the Ship Around! A True Story of Building Leaders by Breaking the Rules by L. David Marquet

The Outstanding Organization: Generate Business Results by Eliminating Chaos and Building the Foundation for Everyday Excellence by Karen Martin

Clarity First: How Smart Leaders and Organizations Achieve Outstanding Performance by Karen Martin

Crucial Conversations: Tools for Talking When the Stakes Are High by Kerry Patterson et al.

Influencer: The Power to Change Everything by Kerry Patterson et al.

The Experience Economy: Work Is Theatre and Every Business a Stage by B. Joseph Pine II and James H. Gilmore

Toyota Kata: Managing People for Improvement, Adaptiveness, and Superior Results by Mike Rother

Toyota Kata Practice Guide: Practicing Scientific Thinking Skills for Superior Results by Mike Rother

Maverick: The Success Story behind the World's Most Unusual Workplace by Ricardo Semler

The Fifth Discipline: The Art and Practice of the Learning Organization, by Peter Senge

Leaders Eat Last: Why Some Teams Pull Together and Others Don't by Simon Sinek

Start with Why: How Great Leaders Inspire Everyone to Take Action by Simon Sinek

Bury My Heart at Conference Room B: The Unbeatable Impact of Truly Committed Managers by Stan Slap

A Company of Leaders: Five Disciplines for Unleashing the Power in Your Workforce by Gretchen Spreitzer and Robert Quinn

The Great Game of Business: The Only Sensible Way to Run a Company by Jack Stack

Mastering the Complex Sale: How to Compete and Win When the Stakes are High! by Jeff Thull

Lean Product and Process Development, 2nd Edition by Allen C. Ward and Durward K. Sobek II

Bonds that Make Us Free: Healing Our Relationships, Coming to Ourselves by C. Terry Warner

A Lapsed Anarchist's Approach to Being a Better Leader by Ari Weinzweig

A Lapsed Anarchist's Approach to Building a Great Business by Ari Weinzweig

A Lapsed Anarchist's Approach to Managing Ourselves by Ari Weinzweig

A Lapsed Anarchist's Approach to the Power of Beliefs in Business by Ari Weinzweig

TED Talks

"The Happiness Advantage" by Shawn Achor, TEDxBloomington

"The Power of Vulnerability" by Brené Brown, TED

"You Need to Foster the Power of Joy" by James Goebel, TEDxTraverseCity

"Super Business Girl" by Asia Newson, TEDxDetroit

"I Know Why You Hate Me," Amanda Grappone Osmer, TEDxAmoskeagMillyard

"How Great Leaders Inspire Action" by Simon Sinek, TEDxPugetSound

Teaching Organizations

Arbinger Institute

Barry-Wehmiller University

Lean Enterprise Institute

Lean Frontiers

VitalSmarts

ZingTrain

Coursera Leadership Course Leading People and Teams Specialization: Leading Effectively. Learn proven management techniques in just four courses.

Stay in touch with us

Keep up with our latest experiments via our monthly newsletters, The Menlo Bits and Joyful Updates.

Sign up on our website: www.menloinnovations.com.

Follow us on Twitter: @menloprez @menloinnovations.

Follow us on LinkedIn.

INDEX

INDEX